DOG TRAINIng 101

Tips and Tricks on How to Completely Train Your Dog

By Adam Young

Table of Content

Chapter 4: Professional training of dog........89

Conclusion........99

Introduction

The book will concentrate primarily on how to train your dog obediently, who can be the perfect companion for people of virtually all ages. This includes all the simple commands a person should teach his or her dog and the dog will enjoy doing it for the owner. Advanced instruction on house and box will also be a part of this fascinating novel. Study your dog's clicker training, teach your dog how to play sports, and get all the help your dog wants. Manage the way they play and work. Long interaction with humans has resulted in dogs being particularly a accustom to the human attitude and being able to survive on a diet comprised on starch which would not be enough for certain canids. Dogs vary greatly in form, size and color. They carry out various human activities, such as herding, hunting, pulling loads, protection, military and police aid, fellowship and, quite lately, helping disabled people and clinical purposes. The impact on humanity has won them the nickname of "A man's best buddy." The dog was the first animal to be tamed, and was selectively bred for specific habits, sensory abilities, and physical characteristics over the centuries. Intelligence of a dog is the dog's ability to interpret information and maintain it as the awareness required to use for problem solving. The dogs were demonstrated to understand by conclusions. A research with Rico demonstrated the he identified more than 200 different things on the labels. By learning exclusion, he deduces the brand of novel objects immediately and even four weeks afterwards the first exposure correctly retrieved certain novel objects. Dogs possess advanced recall skills. A research reported a border collie's understanding and memory skills, "Chaser," which had mastered the names and can identify more than thousand words by verbal command. Dogs are capable of reading and responding properly to the body language of humans like pointing and gesturing, and to fathom voice instructions by humans, however a 2018 review of canid cognitive capabilities concluded that the abilities of dogs are no more remarkable than other species, like chimpanzees, cats or horses. With time, dogs have become a significant part of human households, where they are seldom regarded as mates of work. Unlike 18th century men, today's dog owners treat their dogs as one of their family members and go out of their way to provide the latter with the best of training, diet, grooming and treatment. Perhaps William Koehler was the first dog trainer to have motivated dog owners to communicate closer with their dogs. In fact, dogs were known as working animals before that, and were mostly kept in the backyard. His techniques helped dog owners turn certain animals into domestic dogs. It is he who initiated and demonstrated the importance of the leashes and collars.

Chapter 1: Compliance Training For Puppies and Dogs

When you have recently added a puppy or dog to your family, suggest compliance training to help you and your pet develop a healthy relationship. While training your dog takes patience and determination, it's worth the positive benefits of compliance training.

1.1 The History of The Training of Dog:

No data can be found about explicit training of dog before  the World War 1. Whenever you look at history it's clear why. Many dogs weren't treated as the cherished pets these days and that guide us to conclude that the explicit training of dog that occurs today is not appropriate.

Before World War 1, most of the dogs were culpable family members with serious tasks to do. These dogs were guarding land, providing personal security, herding cattle, riding vermin households, helping in fishing, pulling sleds and carts and finding the lost. Due to the working and living conditions they had inside the family group, the dogs were "trained" humans desired them as well as dogs desired humans. After WWI, though, people began to need dogs to support them in a several other ways. Several dogs had been used to support men in service during battle, resulting in multiple dogs becoming war victims. It prompted the demand for the military to train a large number of dogs to offset the increasingly dwindling service dog supply. The need for quick instruction created the revolution of coercion and the advent of explicit training of dog. This is valid that certain dogs were ready to withstand the training and appear to perform to the high level required, mostly those with a temperament suitable to servicing jobs. However, most of these couldn't handle the extreme demands of training, and therefore their desire to amuse was defeated. Generally, these dogs had been known as weak, unsound or unlearnable. It contributed to the assumption which solely the toughest, most alpha kind of dogs could understand.

When the WWI finished, several military instructors were laid-off from the duties. Both of these instructors were trained in the modern, quick, compulsive methods of training. Throughout this time, individual also started moving from farm work to factory work. This most frequently left the pet dog alone at home to be in trouble. Many masters now felt that they should discipline their dogs due to behaviour issues.

The recently discharged military teachers were easily available at this time, and the whole of society recognized penalty as a legitimate method of training and the notion of compliance-trained family dog by discipline soon caught on. Penal compliance wasn't a new idea. Unfortunately, the pattern that we all taught ourselves on how does social decorum is preserved within communities continues. That enabled it very simple for the typical owner to consent to the methods of compulsion training. Life in after war days was really complicated, and while most people weren't cruel, a commonly known term was the "hard knocks school" Because some people were unable to shine in this challenging habitat, some of the dogs were unable to finish program of obligation training successfully.

The AKC (American Kennel Club) initiated compliance instruction in the U.S in the late 1930's. After WWII, most compliance to competition was performed in society and through compliance organizations approved by the AKC. The after-war techniques of coercion training had gained significant interest in dog societies. Therefore, addiction conditioning was used to teach dogs to compete.

A large number of service dogs had been again needed at the beginning of WWII. To satisfy this need, a lot of young people have been educated how to use training of compulsion to swiftly churn out practical service dogs. Another flood of retired trainers had joined the civil training of dog world by the end of WWII. Increasingly dog masters were working away from home at this time and were having new behavioural issues with their pets. Shortly, the desire for the pet dog to receive explicit training raised, and the accessible instructors were mainly the recently retired army personnel.

Upon the dismissal of Korean War service trainers in the 1950's and Vietnam's Police Intervention in the 1960's, physical and choke chains penalty were commonly used, universally accepted forms of training the dog. It might seem we blame the army for implementing all the harsh methods of training, but that's not true. The notion in our culture that educating is obtained by penalty and that a prize is a payoff unclosed the gateway for the training in compulsions.

When training methods of compliance grew further accessible to the public through books and television in the 1970's and more people began seeking to coach their dogs, many of the stricter training approaches began evolved into lesser unpleasant methods. As a law, most coercion trainers didn't use coercive strategies. By today's norm they were certainly cruel yet some was not violent. Instructor like the Koehler Technique founded by William Koehler have been quite successful. For several different reasons, he was keen to train well-adjusted and very obedient dogs.

Through academic work on wolves, words like "supremacy " had started to surface in training of dogs by the 1980's. Work on wolves was very essential and this research was put to better use by many professional trainers. Sadly, some instructor even claimed, if you didn't dominate your own dog otherwise, he has to control you. This bring to a variety of myths regarding the idea that a dog could not be educated without manipulating him.

While work on operant conditioning was performed in the 1800s, it didn't get into common use until the 1990s. Operant conditioning started to emerge in the training method of clicker about 100 years after the study was performed. Since training based on penalty at this period was so strongly ingrained, training based on clicker was mocked as counterproductive with hard and dominant dogs and coddling the vulnerable and mediocre dogs too. Nevertheless, the movement started to gain momentum when trained by clicker method dogs which feel very low about aggression started to shine in the rings about compliance and competition. Many teachers studied proof of the beneficial results of operating accustom and, examining the advantages of the "recent" form of training, began changing their programs of training.

Training techniques for operant conditioning had acquired fame by 1997, and were commonly used by owners and trainers. Sadly, the techniques and theories of operating accustom were distorted much as with compulsion training. Some trainers assume the conditioning of the operant is 100 per cent positive and the dog isn't right every time. Positive reinforcement is the main teaching technique of operating accustom, however, some correction strategies (check "No Incentive Indicator") are also elements. This is "simply optimistic" belief leads individuals who can't successfully guide dogs do what they desire to do to mark the strategy as unsuccessful and nothing more than the bribery. This is disappointing because it is possible to use operating accustom to train dogs to achieve better outcomes in a larger range of dogs utilizing more humane techniques than ever. Profits even to dog owners. Earlier, they were raised only by dog owners who might mentally or physically intimidate their pets. Operating accustom is a prize-based method of training which means that anybody may learn to master their dogs outside of duress.

1.2 The Starting of training Researchers and Curriculums

Pavlov had been researching reflexive feedback in the dogs in Russia in the early 1900s. Thorndike worked in their own psychology laboratories on the Rule of Effect as well as J.B. Watson promoted a push toward the rigorous empirical behavioral study. Although these persons were establishing the operative accustom foundations, dog instructors were contributing to the advancement of a training technology. Till 1930, Saunders and Walker used an ancient, unconditioned Buick to draw a preview around the country. Hence, individuals might learn how to train their dogs.

Colonel Conrad had raised dogs in Germany and explained their learning habits from the viewpoint of a dog instructor. Most began teaching dogs in police during 1906 and 1912 then he promoted as the director of the state training and breeding organization for the dogs of police in Berlin. Most of them led the Army's Department of Canine Science from 1919 to 1937, and during 1931 he supported to establish the GSAP (German Society for Animal Psychology).

During 1940 decade, Conrad utilized his training expertise to educate the dog trainers and handlers at the Dog Farm in Germany, for unsighted handlers and their dogs.

Most showed a knowledge of operative accustom concepts including secondary and primary reinforcement, forming, chaining and fading almost 28 years prior B.F was written. Skinner's the Species Behaviour. Most defined reinforcement as "the fun feeling when the dog's behavior was right," and distinguished between secondary and primary reinforcer. He indicated to secondary reinforcer as "new encouragement," and utilized his gentle tones and voice a lot in a way most trainers today use clickers.

As with other trainers who come from military or police background, today's trainers will find many of most procedures as "strong handed." However, it is essential to note that a new trainer of dog had identified several of the associations between effects and actions that Skinner could later identify in The Actions of Species, independently. First of the many "how to teach" dog books was probably the 1910 manual Training Dogs.

Josef Weber

Josef arrive from Germany to the USA where he worked as a trainer in the Police Force of Berlin. Josef also developed methods for coaching escort dogs for blind people, in addition to training military and police dogs. Weber became a judge of the AKC (American Kennel Club) and is considered to have a key role in the creation

of the standardized dog compliance tests used in that region. Weber promoted discipline for all dogs, and urged owners to "be proud of the actions of your dog."

William Koehler
William did have some experience with combat dogs, as did Josef Weber and Conrad Most. He instructed dogs as well as their instructor at two California military training centers. Koehler used to be the chief instructor of the OEDC (Orange Empire Dog Club) starting in 1946. This society was renowned for its regularly winning achievements in team contests and for the large number of compliance titles that members won. Koehler and Dick Koehler, his son, have also instructed students in their instructing center. By 1960, they trained more than 40 thousand dogs in classes taught by William or his teachers.

William is accredited with beginning the use in training of short and lengthy series, techniques designed to increase off-leash and attentiveness monitoring. As the in-charge trainer for Walt Disney Studios, with his work on Wildfire, he exposed millions of Americans to the promise of dog compliance training; The Bull Terrier named the brilliant Animal Actor in 1955 for his part in it's a Dog's Life. This distinguished award was awarded to another trained dog by William in 1959, as the best animal actor was named "Chiffon," best familiar to us by title Shaggy Dog.

The Koehler training approach is mainly based on the concepts of punishment and bad reinforcement. Bad reinforcement happens in operative accustoms whenever the frequency of a feedback increases if an aversive occurrence is taken out at once afterwards the response is made. This means that if dog begins to do what you expected him to do after doing something aversive, it gets bad reinforcement from resisting or escaping the cruel stimuli.

The use of the chain coaching or choking chain collar is first of many commonly used forms of bad reinforcement in training of dog. A lot of dogs work hard to stop the jolts after witnessing uncomfortable jolts on the chain. Koehler used choking chains whilst the dog was running ahead or dragging the handler in practices like turning rapidly and heading in the dog's opposite direction.

The use of "throw chains" is a case of discipline in the Koehler system. Koehler utilized bunt chains to restrain dog far away. For instance, When the dog was ordered and failed to react, the chain could be sharply thrown at the rear of the dog. As by Koehler, the trainer is to roll in the rope and make the dog put in front as the chain reaches the horse. Whenever the dog is put on front, William orders the trainers to offer generous applaud, displaying that person trust in rewarding the dogs for correct doings.

In teaching, Koehler recommended encouraging dogs to make mistakes, resulting in penalties for such errors, and instead rewarding desirable behavior. Koehler believed in the use of discipline in situations where as dogs were having behavioral issues like jumping on persons, digging and barking. Punishment, in the scientific sense of the operative accustom, is described as a consequence which makes a unique behavior little likely to happen in the coming days.

Since Koehler began teaching dogs the times have changed. Although he supported his methods throughout his career, many of today's trainers don't find Koehler's punishment procedures acceptable, humane, or fitting. Koehler recommended for digging dogs to dig a pit, fill it by water further place the dog's nose in the mud. Dogs who climb on individuals should obtain a hard knee into

ribs and the dogs who scream loudly should be struck with a belt made of leather according to the Koehler methods.

The pattern shift in training of dog appears to suit shifts that have happened during the years in the care of disabled people and mental issues. Patients in hospitals were diagnosed with shock treatment in the 1960 decade, which regularly used aversive substances like juice of lemon plus ammonia on patients on behavioral problems. It was assumed after that penalty was the easiest, most successful form of addressing a severe issue of behavior. These procedures, with the omission of certain odd cases in specific therapy institutes, aren't being utilized these days and also will be referred as offensive. Usually, training of dog has experienced a change like human therapies, and has moved towards a really good approach.

I had a meeting with William Koehler in the 1980 decade, watching him interact with students and dogs. He seemed to be gentle and caring man then and he obviously loved dogs. He was among the few who known for his willingness to improve difficult dogs at the time Koehler developed his procedures. Koehler had been the only refuge for many puppies. Unless, in a little amount of time, he could not "correct" them, they will be sentenced to death. Although the style in the decades of 1980 & 1990 was towards optimistic training of dog methods, and several of Koehler's practices are being criticized, recognition cannot be denied to Bill Koehler for the huge influence on the training of dog in this region. His book is a classic compliance that lasted for around 50 years and was being utilized to train a large number of dogs.

Blaunce Saunders

Following the remarkable cross-country journey of Blanche Saunders along with Mrs. Helene to sell the advantages for the training of dog to the American nation, Saunders constantly encourage the newly developed sport with religious diligence. Saunders organized compliance shows at high profile gatherings like the Dog Show of Westminster, in the National Week of Dog at the

Rockefeller Center, and with 70,000 fans during intermissions at Yankee Stadium. The Complete Manual on Dog Compliance, was published in 1954. It was the earliest book explicitly written for compliance teachers and in this book, she told the model for practices that could be followed around the country in training of dog classes. Saunders also showed an appreciation of the learning concepts. "Dogs can understand by relating their behavior with a satisfying or frustrating outcome," she said. They need to be punished when doing bad, yet they need to be praised when doing well. "Saunders suggested using disciplinary methods for certain behavioral issues. Whenever dogs growl in training, it told owners to order the dog to act properly. Still, when dog constantly growling, she told that the trainer should keep the leash close and that the dog could be slap tightly across the nose." Bad reinforcement techniques played a central role in the process of Saunders. The choke chain jerking is probably the most commonly used bad reinforcement technique (as a dog tries to escape something aversive). The treatment is legally called punishment whenever a dog gets a jolt by the collar of chain. However, the practice is negative reinforcement as the dog listen the "click" three times of the collar of chain when the instructor gets ready for a punishment, and tries to prevent punishment. In her process, the trainer tells the controllers to teach heeling, "Forward." These students are told to say, "jerk! heel! applaud! " Jolts are also being utilized to teach all habits like sitting-down and address issues like inattention.

Food discipline had been nearly unknown at time when she trained dogs. Saunders believed that dog meal not be offered "like a ransom" on a daily basis, yet also using "a bit at this moment and after to solve a problem" was appropriate. This was probably the starting of the change far away from military and police training strategies that focused mainly on punishment, evasion, and habits of avoidance. Specifically, such approaches suggested that trainers would not be using dog meals in training. She used affirmation and pats mainly as reinforcer. Saunders also employed physical reminders to coach new talents. Having the master move on the short rope, dogs were instructed to "sit" While training dogs to "wait," handlers would place pressure on the shoulder of the dog to drive the dog into certain position. She has made a number of important advancements to training of dog. She was first of many compliance teacher's trainers and moreover she was a pioneer in early seminar. Her book told a highly detailed weekly training plan for novices by next level dog compliance classes. She got herself respect and compassion. Saunders was probably the first writer to consistently emphasize the reinforcement importance in training, thereby beginning the movement towards the optimistic methods of training used these days.

Milo Pearsall
The 1958 book Dog Compliance Training, by Milo Pearsall, was marketed as a book that changes training of dog with a gentler approach. Some of the teaching strategies used by Pearsall used to be same bad reinforcement approaches identified by Saunders 4 years before. When teaching heeling, Pearsall utilized grabbing on leash as a punishment, to force the dog to lay down, and to maximize focus.

Pearsall used methods for punishing inappropriate habits. Pearsall suggested that the individual knee in the ribs of dog to correct dogs which jump on people. Masters were asked to bind a stick to a small rope swinging from the collar to avoid car chasing. The stick struck the dog's forelegs if dog tried to chase. Pearsall recommended that people move their dog's noses outside the incident for housebreaking incidents, thus the dog might understand the sense of what's wrong. Dogs that ran away from a line were educated in the Pearsall system. They were jolted off their feet as they tried to run along lengthy rope bind to collars.

In year 1958, knowledge of Pavlov's accustom work, which had been finished just some decades ago, Pearsall did write, "At first the dog gets his lessons by applying a proper stimulus pressuring him for sitting, for instance at the same moment a second stimuli, he is given orders. Soon, secondary means just the same as primary means to him. The very known instance of this transition is Pavlov's famous experiment on dog salivation. "Sadly, although Pearsall understood there was a link between training of dog and learning theory, he muffled the principles of response conditioning along with operative (learning) conditioning. Dog learning is simply a case of operative accustom whenever a stimulus is pushing the dog into rest has been combined with the order, "sit"

Dogs are wonderful animals, and always learn amid the frustrating messages we can send. Pearsall said that the dog would be kicked under the jaw (with the fingers) for serious offences. When the dog was hit for wrong doing, he told the trainer to immediately praise the dog. Behaviorally, we all know that issuing a reinforcer straight after a punisher does not make sense. Such a combination will obviously result in the punisher claiming improving qualities.

The reinforcer (praise) should not be given until the dog has participated in appropriate actions according to sound behavioral principles. That behavior, then, will be improved. Pearsall explained praising as soon as you disciplined by saying that the trainer had to "let the dog know he was still loved" and that the trainer was on the side of the dog.

The word "punishment" in operant conditioning is a technical scientific term that means providing a consequence that will make a specific action less likely to occur in the future. For example, if you grabbed the handle into a new pan in which you cooked and you were badly burned, you were punished in operational terms for grabbing the handle of this pan while cooking. Most dog trainers think of "punishment" as having a particular purpose, from years past to the current moment. We associate it with a crime, retribution, or a person just trying to get even.

Pearsall, like many trainers, did not use the operant conditioning definition of punishment. He thought trainers should "bear in mind that the dog is never disciplined as a first rule in compliance training, too. He's changed. He doesn't understand punishment, and will never understand it. "Pearsall used the" crime "form of punishment, here on the dog, a distinction entirely missed.

Dog compliance training was a very complete piece of work. In addition to offering general training material at all stages of teaching, it provided information on choosing dogs, retraining, and box training. Pearsall was a highly regarded judge and professor in compliance at the AKC. Pearsall's teaching techniques have trained hundreds of thousands of puppies. Pearsall was an early advocate of "kindergarten puppy classes." These puppy classes were mainly intended to educate parents and promote socialization among the puppies. Pearsall emphasized that these lessons would be enjoyable and that they should not be formal training exercises that would restrict puppies the freedom to behave as friendly, cheerful, puppet explorers. Milo Pearsall was perhaps best known for the national workshops and clinics he held in order to encourage training of dog and his ability to show how easily dogs learn in the hands of a professional trainer using problem dogs (from the audience).

Winifred Strickland

During decade of 1940, Winifred had begun training in dog compliance. She retired from competition in 1955, just around the time that Saunders and Pearsall inspired with their seminars on trainers. One of the first "best trainers" was Strickland, an AKC compliance judge. She won 160 compliance titles, 40 perfect scores, 30 service titles, three compliance trial championships, five national compliance championships, five tracking titles, plus hundreds of top awards. Strickland described a sequenced resume for novices by practical instruction in her 1965 book Expert Compliance Training for Dogs. She said her system would yield dogs ready to work. Strickland used snap-release punishments to practice heeling and "practice the dog how to act." When dogs ignored orders, she would give them a quick nose tap. She used the widely used technique of a knee in the dog's chest for dogs that jumped on people. She used verbal reprimands on when the dog had an incident in housebreaking puppies, and she praised the dog as it was removing from outside. He agreed that discipline would also be applied immediately when Strickland needed to correct the dog and the lesson proceeded so the dog could do it right and get rewarded. Strickland emphasized the value of a good timing in both punishment and praise given. Strickland used physical cues to do "down" instruction. She pulled the dog's front legs out as she lowered it down and said, "Down, good down." Strickland slowly faded her control of the dog to drop the dog down at a distance by beginning the training with the dog a short distance away and gradually raising the distance. Strickland instructed her young dogs to use the food as an opportunity to perform tricks. She explained how she would mix food with praise and the dogs finally worked solely for praise (conditioned reinforcement). Unlike most other coaches of her day, Strickland counseled not to use food in preparation. She said the use of food "is a cruel approach to training and would only work for dogs who think more about their own stomachs than of their owners." Despite this statement, Strickland explained in Expert Compliance Training for Dogs how food may be used to teach advanced skills such as the "go-out" exercise for compliance. This exercise includes taking the dog away from the handler, being told to sit down and then jumping over a specified hurdle. Strickland would put tiny bits of food at the location the dog was being guided to. The dog would rush out to get food and Strickland would give a verbal warning for the dog to settle down. The food would slowly disappear from the training and the dog would run out to the location when given a verbal order.

A number of leading trainers in the 1960's claimed dogs trained to prepare for formal compliance would stay in kennels. The thought was that the dogs would be so delighted to have a human touch they would be able to work with. Strickland was not in agreement with the kenneling dogs. She believed dogs should behave "as family members" in the household. She cited several examples of how her German Shepherds exercised their training during the day by retrieving objects and carrying out certain practical tasks. Praise was an "integral part" of Strickland's training approach and she encouraged trainers to "continually try to instill a sense of pleasure in your training to keep your dog excited about it." Winifred Strickland was responsible for a significant advance in the movement for the more humane childhood training of dogs. Reply Strickland, "Don't be ashamed if anyone overhears that you're praising your puppy. Be proud of that, "it tells us how much training of dog has come in the last 30 years.

Kryon Pryor

Pryor has been a pioneer in science, researcher, animal trainer, and seminar. Pryor also played an important role for dog trainers in the 1980s and 1990s as a translator of basic behavioral principles for those who work in the animal care field. Before the 1980s, Pryor used to be a marine trainer of mammal who utilized concepts of Skinner for operating accustom to educate dolphins and produce mammal demonstration in marines. She published her book Do not kill the Dog in 1984, a user-friendly, influential description of operating procedures for the public at large. Pryor utilized real-world scenarios in Don't Shoot the Dog to illustrate how operational techniques can be used to alter the actions of one's children, partner, neighbor, or pets. When Reader's Digest released an excerpt of Don't Shoot the Dog with its readership of more than 20 million readers, many behavior experts were ecstatic that someone had effectively applied operant conditioning to the general public. At the Association for Behavior Analysis International Conference in the late 1980s, Pryor gave the keynote address to behavioral scientists, and the connection between science and modern training of dog was created. The training materials and seminars given by Pryor demonstrated how operating procedures can be used to provide effective training. With her "shaping game" and examples of "clicker training,"

Pryor also introduced trainers to ideas such as secondary reinforcement. By the mid-1990s many dog trainers were writing and holding regional workshops on how to use clickers in training. Numerous dog trainers gave seminars and written on subjects related to operant conditioning, such as positive reinforcement, influencing attitudes, and raising undesirable behaviors. The long-term influence these trainers have on the training of dog industry is still unknown.

Understanding the whole dog
In the years before operant conditioning was a concept common to dog trainers, well-known trainers with a steady regularity developed new training techniques or variations to the old ones. Notwithstanding an increasingly increasing number of books and seminars on "how to learn," top trainers have known for decades that more is required to train a dog than a series of techniques or trick bags.

1.3 Compliance training and its Types:

Dogs are social animals with natural instinctual behaviors for the breed. Compliance training for dogs is also required in order to reduce the inherent tendency of a dog to annoy your neighbors, home or family and acclimatize the dog to daily routines. Many points are required when teaching a dog to avoid excessive chewing, barking, jumping, and biting, and there are a variety of different ways to effectively accomplish this task. Beat, spank or otherwise put your hands on your dog should never be done with proper compliance training. Easy voice commands and positive reinforcement have proven highly successful, regardless of age or breed of the dog.

1. Puppy Training

When necessary, dog compliance training will start in the puppy stage. If training is carried out properly when a dog is 3 to 6 months old, standard commands will be in place and the puppy will grow up into an adult dog that is sociable, polite and well-behaved. Puppy training usually requires regular lessons that teach ordinary commands like coming, heel, sitting, staying and off. This should teach the puppy how to move correctly when indoors, outside and in social environments. Puppies will also need to practice home-training to avoid unpleasant messes in your house. Equally significant, when puppies are going through the teething period, they need to chew to help reinforce the teeth and relieve the teething pain. Proper training and rewards of suitable chew toys will help discourage the puppy from trying to chew on and ruin your furniture, shoes or other household objects. Puppy compliance training courses can also include socialization, hygiene and proper feeding.

2. Compliance Training for Adult Dogs

Compliance training for dogs over the age of six months may involve lessons containing any of the regular commands such as basic puppet training, which can also include extra instruction for dogs with violent behavior, social problems, or other particular problem areas. Adult training of dog that goes beyond the simple methods that require more advanced techniques and you should always opt for the lessons to be active and present, so that the dog learns to trust and obey you as the owner. The dog's age doesn't matter if correct training and technique are put into action. Short and easy instructions, meaningful reinforcement and discipline tend to be key points in incorporating the most appropriate approaches for any course in dog compliance.

3. Special Training of dog

Including standard dog compliance training, there are also several advanced courses required to train dogs interested in other professions or events. Police, rescue, and search dogs are likely to need a passing grade in simple compliance training and then move on to more rigorous, profession-specific training. This also refers to dogs interested in supporting the needs of the elderly, disabled or children. Specialization for AKC or other dog show entries or courses designed to teach those tricks and behaviors for entertainment purposes that require event preparation.

4. Vocational Training

Much like humans, dogs are able to learn a wide range of skills. There are dogs learning how to herd, hunt, perform search and rescue work, support the elderly or even work with law enforcement agencies. In reality, these skills are like occupational training for dogs as it will mean they will have a job that will benefit people in some way. Dogs learn very unique strategies in these classes to refine their senses and interact with people but the classes are often intensive and time-consuming. Any form of the training of dog would suggest they have a strong base in terms of their basic skills. Many of such systems are also appropriate for different breeds.

Dogs are truly incredible creatures because they can easily go beyond simple compliance training and save lives in reality. Both dogs will learn regardless of their history, but due to their physical characteristics certain abilities would be easier for different breeds. As long as you can find a trained coach to train your puppy, the sky is the limit.

5. Agility Training

Agility training is for dogs, including obstacle courses, running, or jumping, that can compete in dog sports. It is certainly a more sophisticated form of training that implies the dog already knows the basic commands. In the game, the trainer is not permitted to contact or praise the dog so there will need to be a clear link between the owner and the dog through voice and physical movements. Although it's true that any dog will master these skills, some breeds are better suited to these activities than others.

1.4 Choosing a Master for Training

Most of the schools are willing to encourage you to visit and experience one or two class to certain about the style of teaching suits your values (leave the canid at house for this). Almost all dogs can grasp best by positive support training; praise the dog for the correct choice and denying rewards, or neglect the dog for the incorrect choice. Take care of the dogs while attending a class, are they appear to be glad? Relaxing? Excited for the job? Is the coach getting dogs and masters encouraged? Is the class

apparently working in a healthy and efficient way? When you're not feeling confident at a specific training facility, neither will your dog, so you'll set your own dog to lose. Continue to look for an institution where you have relief both your dog and yourself would do happier at this setting.

Behaviorist vs Trainer
There are several significant distinctions to observe among behaviorists and trainers. Behaviorists may be veterinarians and/or trainer. Trainers are trained to treat

symptoms, but the root causes of symptoms are not necessarily. For example, teaching certain habits and becoming accustomed with a dog to be alone will help to reduce the anxiety about separation. Nonetheless, the main cause would possibly demand to be identified by the behaviorist and whom would then be able to direct you to a therapist if she or he could not deal with the issues during training. Many teachers are accredited by organizations or schools in the classroom. Reviewing your trainer's certifications, or reviewing recommendations if your instructor is not accredited, is also wise. One class of dog-training practitioners is the AKC CGC (Canine Good Citizen) examiners. These examiners can or cannot be behaviorists or trainers yet are accredit by AKC in the CGC exam to assess dogs. For example, teaching certain habits and changing a dog accustomed to be alone will help to reduce the anxiety about separation. Nonetheless, the main cause would possibly demand to be identified by the behaviorist and who would then be able to direct you simply to an instructor if she or he could not deal with the issues during training.

The Puppy Socializing

The area of debate that is sometimes ignored include toileting and handling. When your mentor gives sound guidance and you obey her instructions, you'll be praised by your groomer and veterinarian. By the young age of dog, practice handling and grooming your dog and your groomer and veterinarian would not have any difficulty inspecting, bathing, clipping or treating him. Nevertheless, if the only chance your dog observes a brush or nail clippers is on the groomer or veterinarian, he would possibly be on terms with things that are frightening or unpleasant. When you begin at your home the place your dog is relaxed, you may build the experiences of grooming and vetting far more enjoyable for both. Also, as a gift several groomers cost less for handling the easy dogs, as they may be trained without a second groomer's assistance. Here's what we will do. If she is too big to bear, take your puppy places — by car, in your arms or in a child's wagon. Take her to a supermarket, a hardware store, bus station, railway station, if possible, on a train. Take her to a gas station, florist, and auto body shop. Step into the waiting room for the vet and back out. Visit the park, the dairy, the construction site and the police station. Encourage her to wrestle between rocks and logs. Let her experience many underfoot textures, from grass to asphalt to leaves to gratings made of metal. Teach her to use stairs from the lowest level and work your way up until she can easily, up and down, navigate a whole staircase.

Introduce your puppy to the world's every kind of people. Our nation remains culturally and racially divided. Many of the customers have admitted to me with shame that their dog responds negatively to people of races other than their own. So, make a particular statement about being multicultural. Bring any quality dry dog food. Encourage friendly kids to pet your dog and put a treat on him. People who use wheelchairs and walkers, truck drivers for delivery, deep-voiced bearded men, nuns, homeless people collecting bottles from the street — none of these common people would be special to your dog. The same is true of wildlife. A puppy growing up loving cats is less likely when he grows up to view them as predators. When you live in the country, access to other domestic animals can easily come; when you live in the city, you can deal with what you have — police horses can be seen from a distance, and combined with tidbits if your puppy is skittish about them. As with other puppies, just screen them! Your puppy will meet friendly and happy dogs and puppies which you know for a fact. A well-run class or play group on puppy manners would improve. But well run dog parks should be avoided before the vaccine is complete. Lots of dogs are terrified of unfamiliar sounds. Make sure your dog listens to police sirens, fire engines, the constant beep that makes a truck when it's backup. Birdsong, songs, steel rolling windows, irritating ringtones. Doorbells, intercoms, crashing pots and pans. Gunfire and similar sharp, cracking sounds are often the culprits of dog phobias; download free internet recordings and one day plays them as background music. Say you're introducing your puppy with dark glasses and headdress to a friend and your puppy is shying away. Relax, take a deep breath and let your puppy withdraw. Tell your friend to lie down over the puppy and forget. Let your pup proceed at his own pace, and your friend doesn't pay him any attention. Softly and warmly praise the dog as he explores. Stop luring him out with food — it's necessary to stay in his comfort zone. When he relaxes absolutely next to your mate, she will be able to give him a treat; if that goes well, then a script comes next. Do not push — just repeat the meeting later on another day if your puppy remains a little skittish.

For something or someone your puppy doesn't take in step, follow the same pattern: let him withdraw to a distance where he feels safe, and then move forward in his own good time. Praise but don't tempt his courage.

If you find that in certain situations or by certain types of people, your puppy is easily spooked, speak to a behavior professional right away. Early action is always particularly malevolent and the sooner you interfere in any future issues, the better the chances of solving them.

Chapter 2: Basic Commands to teach to your Dog

This chapter will be mostly related to teach basic commands to your dog. It will be concerned about teaching them how to sit, stand, lay down on the floor, stay, to leave, and to go away for picking some object.

2.1 Basic Instructions for a Dog to be trained:

1. How to Teach a Dog to Sit Down?
There are probably two different ways to show your puppy what "sitting" means. The first method is called grab. Stand up in front of your puppy with some food or tidbits for his son. Wait for him to sit down-say "yes" and have a treat for him. Then step back or sideways to allow him to stand and wait before he sits down. Give them another treat while they're down. You should start saying "down" right after a few repetitions, as he starts to down. The next choice is luring. Have your puppy down, keep a treat as a lure. Place the treat right in front of the pup's nose and then raise the food gradually over his mouth. He is likely to sit up as he raises his head at the treat to nibble. When his bottom hits the table, encourage him to eat the treat. Continue with the food lure once or twice, then remove the food and use only your empty hand, but keep rewarding the puppy until he sits down. You should start saying "down" right before you send the hand signal, until he knows the hand signal to sit down. Always put your puppy physically in the sitting position; some dogs can be confused or upset about this.
2. How to Teach a Dog to Stay?
The puppy who knows the "wait" cue will stay sitting before you ask him to get up by offering another cue,

called the "release term." The goal is to teach your dog to stay sitting until you give the release cue, then start adding distance. First of all, teach the word release. Choose the word you're going to use, like "OK" or "free." Sit up in a sit or sit with your dog, throw a treat on the floor, and say your word as he moves forward to get the treat. Do this a few times before you can first say the word and then throw away the treat before it starts going. This shows the dog that turning your feet means the release cue. When your dog is familiar with the release cue and how to sit on the cue, put it in a sit, turn to face it, to give it a treat. Stop, and give him a special treat to remain in a sit, and then release him. The time you wait between treatments rises slowly (it will help you sing the ABC's in your head and work your way up the alphabet). When your dog is jumping up before the release cue, that's all right! It just means that he's not prepared to stay for so long so you can make things easier by going back to a shorter time. You will start adding distance until your dog will stay in a sit for several seconds. Place him in a sitting room and say "stay," take a step back, then step back to the pup, offer a treat and let go of your word. Continue building in stages, holding your dog pretty easy to stay productive. Practice both facing him and walking away with your back turned (which is more realistic). You can slowly raise the gap until your dog can stay there. That's true for the "rest," too. The more firmly he knows it, the longer he can rest. The trick to this is not to expect too much, too soon. Training targets are gradually accomplished, so you may need to calm down and concentrate on one thing at a time. Sessions will be quick and effective in ensuring that the instruction "sticks."

3. How to teach a Dog to Lay Down?

"Down" can be taught very similarly to "sitting." You can wait for your dog to lie down (starting in a dull, small room such as a bathroom can help) and catch the action by rewarding your dog with a reward while he's lying down, giving him his release cue to stand up (and lure if needed) and then waiting for him to lie down again. After standing up, as he is lying down easily, you should start saying "down" right before he does. You may also lure a down from a sit or stand by catching the dog's nose with a treat in your hand and gradually lowering it to the floor. Give the treat when the elbows of the dog touch down to start the floor. When he can follow your hand signal consistently, start saying "down" as you move your head. Just like sitting, never put your dog in a down using intimidation.

4. How to teach your Dog or Puppy not to bite you?
It is very essential for all the dogs to learn how to control the impact of a bite. A time might come when they're in terror or pain, and they're putting their face on you or may on someone else. Yet if they have mastered the resistance of bite, they realize they shouldn't bite hard. Obviously, the puppies nip each other when playing. The other dog would probably make a loud yelp sound if puppies bite very strongly on their mom or littermate, alerting them, "Hey it hurts! "You can also teach this, depending on the dog, by creating a highly pitched sound of "ow!" When they are biting you, be on alert as this really gets them worked up even more with some of the puppies, and is possibly to bite you. In this situation, to calm down, it's best to turn around quickly, move away or bring the dog gently into their box for some minutes. Make sure to feed the dog with a tidbit and some positive encouragement, when they back off.

5. Teaching your Dog, Meaning of Biting is 'Game Over'
When playing, in case the puppy start biting you that means playing time is over, without exceptions. Physically abusing or yelling at puppy is actually a kind of reward, as weird as it sounds. It teaches them that the biting is getting some form of reaction from you is called bad reinforcement. That may also able them to afraid of being dealt with. Teach them, then, that scratching won't get them anywhere. Kathy Santo, the dog columnist and trainer for the Family Dog of AKC writer, recommends going back and wrapping your hands inside the armpits. "It's actually a soothing signal as well as a slight removal of concentration," she stated "And beware not to play rough with the young puppy in certain ways that just allow them to bite you or lose control." It's a great thought to have a puppy bite toy closely always, so you may predict biting action and replace the toy with furniture or hand. By doing so, the pups will learn what's okay to chew or bite. In case they begin toying with your toes or fingers during playing, then give a treat. In case they keep nipping, then immediately interrupt the play period. If you've taught the puppy to sit down, you could even encourage them by ordering them to sit with a toy and be rewarded. Stop the jumping. In case the puppy pounces on your feet or legs as you're walking, a typical playful puppy action, Santo suggests keeping a great-value reward along your leg while you move, to help your puppy teach walking alongside you. Use the same technique while training a dog to move on a rope. Place them in a break time. Place the puppy gently in their box to allow them a chance to settle down and to protect puppies from biting. Making sure they don't begin to equate the box with punishment is really important so be cool. You should let them out, until

the pup settles down. Give them some potty or silent time break. A biting habit of puppy is a very exhausted puppy sometimes and also, they want to be placed in a silent room or box to sleep. They might want a potty break or simply thirsty or hungry. Use some resources to help. If the puppy continues chewing, he can only need to waste mental or physical strength even after you change a toy

multiple time. Bring them in the lawn, and see them playing around. Strengthen the ideal behaviors. We often forget that we should boost them with a "nice doggy" or patting or a part of kibble when our puppy is relaxed and quiet. Through positive reinforcement you can help them understand what habits you're looking for. Don't strike the dog. Don't ever strike or physically abuse your dog otherwise. In case your pup appears to be chewing out of frustration, ask a dog trainer or veterinarian about approaches to handle the attitude.

Cavaletti Activities for The Dog at Home

A long walk isn't an option cavaletti will help burn off physical and mental energy. In case you have limited time and room, these movements of "little horse" may just be your thing. Cavaletti strengthens the muscles, stimulates the brain and support creating the bond between the dog owners. Stashed in your wardrobe, kitchen or garage, you can have an amazing canid conditioning secret. His name cavaletti which sounds just like something with some meatballs and marinara sauce that will come in. In fact, it's an Italian name meaning "little horse." These trainers created Cavaletti activities for horse training, like moving over beams variations. This method for dog sport activities and physical treatment spread into the canine world. The mechanism comprises of beams which are positioned near the base. Foam pool noodles, PVC piping, low agility jumps, balanced golf clubs on shoes (tennis) or cones can be used to create it. Cheap cavaletti sets are also available that you can purchase online. Cavaletti uses a number of doses to work on canine conditioning. You can function distinct group of muscles by altering the configurations of the beams. The size of the beams and their height motivates your dog to travel in various ways. Apparently endless formats exist, and the variety boost body coordination, pace, flexibility, strength and stamina. "Dogs utilize barely of their usable joint variety of movement for other gaits, like trotting and walking," stated by Darryl Millis who is DVM, orthopedic surgery professor and founder of the UTCVM's Veterinary Sports Medicine Center. "The dog, like in cavaletti that steps over obstacles increases the bending of particular joints. It facilitates a larger active range of muscle strength and movement across a wider range. Furthermore, sense of the joint positioning and body awareness are tested by moving over obstacles, particularly when there are distinct configurations and rail heights. "The cavaletti in zigzag patterns or spaced near together improve the ability of a dog to shorten or gather their move. Such ability makes changing course or reducing speed easier for a dog. For example, in case the dog can move rapidly, they can change their direction efficiently on a swiftness course. Cavaletti can also be a crucial part of ensuring the physical fitness and balance for a dog to leap. Cavaletti starts in a direct line will increase pace by extending a dog's move. The gradual introduction of space among the beams helps to lengthen the trip, as the dog need to walk forward to avoid the beams. Haste is of great benefit to sporting and servicing dogs also think of police K-9s agility dogs or following suspects. Cavaletti will intensify the rush just before the jumping, for a more effective dock diver. "These activities are ideal for the dogs with neurological or orthopedic problems, or healing from multiple accidents or operations, but also for servicing dogs or athletes to keep their bodies healthy," Millis stated. Instructor use many configurations to reinforce the various body pieces. You may begin by choosing more than one of those 4 activities 3 to 5 days in a week to complement your dog's fitness routine. Set the beams very low, around hock (angle) lower or higher, for the first 4 exercises. Strive to reach 3 to 5 sets of 3 to 10 repetitions. This version takes its name from the game that originated in China in the 1800s. It lay out a collection of random small sticks. Put your beams in a random way and make sure your dog has enough room among the beams to guide whilst trotting or walking. The beams have to be 2 inches wide or lower. Place the beams on the ground for little dogs, or for a simple setup! How to do it: Go down the row of beams during moving with the dog then go back one rep. Have the dog walk around an obstacle (cone) a few feet far from the first stick and last stick for an extra challenge. Square Design, position 4 beams in a linking square, and four cones. How to do it: Lead your dog by jumping over the beams with your own body movement in figure of 8 walking style round the cones. Vary the figure of 8 style to the cones and neighboring cones crosswise. Take 4 cone wraps as one repeat. Setup Serpentine, Initially, connect 3 to 5 beams, to create a direct line between 4 cones. Then take a number of even beams and position them on opposite cone sides. They would walk a serpentine or zigzag path when the dog was to move over all the beams. How to do it: move alongside the dog and show arm signals for the twisty motion. Your dog must weave among the cones as she steps over each wire. Back and down across the serpentine is only one rep. Setup of High Steps, arrange 4 or 6 beams at the elbow or lower, height of your dog, and around twelve inches away. How to do it: Move behind the dog and allow them to move with confidence around the high beams. Go back and repeat to finish one rep. Position 4 or 6 beams between 2 cones end by extending a stride setup. The among between each beam will be the height (topmost position of the shoulders) of the dog at the withers. When your own dog has a lengthy neck, instead of the withers scale, you can utilize their spine — without the tail—. How to do it: move alongside the dog to enable them to trot or move over the beams. You need your dog to move between beams with one hindlimb and one forelimb, to lengthen the speed of your dog, raise the gap among the beams by one inch only! You'll put another inch among the beams and so on, as they intensify their movement over time.

How to handle older dogs?

Santo teaches dogs at her Kathy Santo Training of dog School in New Jersey for home life and competition. She is the author of Kathy Santo's Dog Sense and has worked with many winners of the Compliance court. She also teaches on-line streaming dog-training courses. I didn't understand how that was possible when I first learned the phrase "old dogs are the best puppies." What could a young dog's drive, excitement, and boundless energy ever compare to a low-key, laid-back senior? Here are some important lessons that I learned from my first dog, Opal, when she came into her golden years. Senior Isn't "Small".

Yet when I told her to go out for a walk, fetch, or do compliance training, she complied with it joyfully and enthusiastically. While I was working, she was as content to cuddle down on the couch next to me as she was going to be involved. This does not mean the end of learning, either. While we were transitioning from compliance to retirement from competition, her desire to know and communicate with me remained. She mastered all the' human' tricks that I never taught her before the last few months of her life, happily and easily because I'd become more focused on the precision and motivation of what we had to do in the ring at trials. Senior citizens are our historians.

I was married Opal was with me, had my son, and when we moved. These were milestones in my life, and with each of them having her by my side built a bond that was at the heart of our love for each other. Yet there comes a caveat for such advantages to older dogs. There are a few slip-ups and mistakes which should be avoided, popular among older dog owners. This way, the canine senior citizen does not experience behavior problems unexpectedly late in life. Don't let Rules relax. The Requirements are relaxed.

- Golden Retriever has age 10. Before he gets a treat, he always has to wait until he goes through the doors and before he can get something I've thrown. Regardless of his generation, the "ask for permission" mentality isn't eliminated. However, if he had faced arthritis or had any other physical condition, the rules would be updated. So, for instance, if he couldn't sit and wait comfortably he could still stand and wait. Naughty activity pops up from nowhere. I hear tales of woe every week at my dog school about a previously great adult dog, which reportedly started stealing food off tables, counters and plates "out of the blue." Yet when I dig a little deeper, I hear stories of the owners who could not resist the cute, old face of their dog. The consequence is owners who offer the dog food from the bowl, the counter and the pan. The behavior of a dog is also a product of its owners. All. Simple. It's time. Age Isn't an Excuse "We won't live forever" is not an excuse to break the rules of the house and let your dog steal shoes, knock down people and beg at table. There are other forms in which you can offer extra incentives that match their senior status without your dog being a canine criminal. I'm not Machiavellian about this now mind. It's special to allow your senior dog to come up on the sofa, or climb up on you, or even enjoy the last bits of your dinner from your plate (it happens!) because you gave him permission to continue. Yet when a dog takes what he wants, a pushy dictator emerges, and no one wants to deal like that. Now, please excuse me while I give my senior dog, Indy, a belly rub, which was lying next to me on the sofa, eviscerating the new stuffed toy I gave him to keep him busy while I was finishing this section. Better boy Indy!

How to prevent Dog from Stealing Food?
Is your dog onto the counter with his nose?
Dogs are "counter-surfers," which means they see what kind of food they can grab from any variety of locations, even directly off your table.

A dog tries to steal food, when he succeeds; he discovers he gets a reward that only reinforces the action. Sure that will make it tough to break the habit— but it's not impossible.

What would you do to avoid this kind of behavior, as a dog owner? Kathy Santo, dog trainer and AKC Family Dog columnist, suggests the following when working with a counter-surfing puppy. Delete the opportunity; make sure there's nothing on the counter (not even crumbs). "I call this the Impact of an Empty Bird Feeder," says Santo. "When you stop filling a bird feeder, the birds finally stop coming back." If you have to keep food on your counter (a pie to cool, for instance, or a spread for a party), keep the dog out of the kitchen using a baby gate, or place a box in it or behind a shut door.

Food in basenji: When you see him sniffing around in the kitchen, instead of yelling at him or punishing him, tell him to go to his place and recompense him with a tasty Purina ® Pro Plan ® reward for compliance. He will soon know that the chance of having a treat is higher when he listens to it compared to eating a snack behind your back. Still, even though your dog is being taught, try to keep those counters and coffee tables clean and watchful. "If you leave the room with a lure on your desk, there are some dogs that, no matter how well trained they are, may have a momentary error of judgment," Santo says. Teach him to leave it; "leave it" is another important order to teach your dog. This way, if you catch him attempting to get anything he shouldn't have (or he can get it), using "leave it" would deter him from eating it. It is especially relevant if your dog has deprived him of something potentially harmful.

1. How to prevent your dog from counter-snuffing?

Few dogs sparked a fire in their home this week in Central Pennsylvania attempting to steal a box of cupcakes left on the counter by the owner. Thankfully, the landlord of the owner dropped by the apartment to let the dogs go outside and saw the explosion, the Associated Press reported. Police concluded that the dogs flipped the knobs onto the stove in an effort to access the tidbits. Counter-surfing does not always cause such a dramatic impact, but it is a mischievous activity which dog owners should not tolerate. It's a self-rewarding behavior, implying, as stated in this book, that if the dog succeeds, he gets a treat (like a cupcake), which just reinforces the action. That makes it difficult to practice against. Yet this isn't impossible. Kathy Santo, an AKC Family Dog trainer and author, advises the following when working with a counter-surfing puppy: take away the chance, make sure nothing (not even crumbs) is on the table. "I call this the Impact of an Empty Bird Feeder," says Santo. "When you stop filling a bird feeder, the birds finally stop coming back." If you have to keep food on your counter (a pie to cool, for instance, or a spread for a party), keep the dog out of the kitchen using a baby gate, or place a box in it or behind a shut door.

Him for fighting, teach your dog to "go to his place." Instead of yelling at him or punishing him, tell him to go to his place and praise him for compliance, if you see him sniffing in the kitchen. He will soon learn that, when he listens to you, the chance of having a treat is better than when he sneaks a snack behind your back. Still, even though your dog is being taught, try to keep those counters and coffee tables clean and watchful. "When you leave the room with a temptation on your desk, there are certain dogs who, no matter how well trained they are, may have a momentary error of judgment," Santo says.

1. How to train your Dog to Play Dead?

Playing dead is a very smart game for dogs. While it is not as critical as training your dog to follow commands such as "wait" and "stop," it is not hard to train most dogs to play dead. This can be a fun game for both the dog and its audience. What you need is a couple of his favorite tidbits, and you're able to get your dog conditioned to play dead. For a clicker this is also a nice trick to practice. When you want to go the training path with a clicker, make sure your clicker is handy.

Start in a Down Position, if your dog is not yet lying on order, go back and focus on that before you start playing it to death. Give a treat, keep a treat close to the nose of your dog, and slowly turn it over to its side to get it. It helps if your dog already knows how to turn over, because the motion of turning on its side will already be familiar. Reward Listening, Say "yes" or "no" as soon as your dog lies on its side. Or, click on your clicker. Instead, make a treat for the puppy. Repeat many times on those moves. Attach a Signal, and then attach a trigger word and a hand gesture after the dog has performed the action a few times. Most people tend to use the verbal "bang" order, along with a hand gesture order, holding their fingers to look like a dog-pointing pistol. Some tend to simply use "dead." You can of course use whatever word and hand signal you want. Some people tend to say a funny word, like this: "Would you rather be a cat or would you rather be dead?" It's fun to see a dead dog play with that one. Offer word and hand signal for the chosen cue, then repeat steps. Practice this trick for a few minutes each time several times a day and it will not be long before your dog falls to its side in response to your signal. Problems and Proofing Behaviors, when your dog already knows how to turn over, it may have a natural tendency to go all the way over when you try to tempt him to his side. It's a wonderful time taking your clicker out to catch the exact action that you want. Lure your dog with a treat to her hand, immediately click on your clicker and give the dog a treat. If it is trying to avoid turning over, walk a minute away. When your dog is aware that the reward will vanish when it rolls over full, it will most likely stop doing so, and instead show the action that gives the reward. If you're having trouble getting your dog to obey the reward and it ends up sitting on her side, then you should show what you want her to do. Using the treat as a lure and, at the same time, you can move it to his side very gently. Press your clicker (or tell him "yes" or "well") and give her a treat as soon as the dog is in the correct place. If your dog leaps faster than you like from playing dead, you should teach them to stay down there longer. Rather of giving the dog a treat the minute it's lying on her side, wait a couple of seconds and then offer the treat. Practice it a couple of times, then add a few seconds. In this way you can add more time slowly before your dog lies down and stays dead for a few minutes or more. When your dog makes more than two or three mistakes in a row at any point in the training, chances are you've gone on too fast. Go back a step or two and practice, and then start going slowly forward again when the dog is good at that stage. Remember to be honest and cautious. Each dog learns at a different rate. If your dog is upset, exhausted or bored, keep optimistic training sessions and end the session. Always try to end sessions on a positive note, even if the last thing you do is turn to a simpler behavior like "down" or "down."

2.2   Some other Advanced Training

How to Train the Dog to Turn Back to his Place?

May be a good approach to teach your dog to go to his place when you need to calm down or get out of under your feet? You can choose one place in your home or another in each room to take your dog when you tell him to come to his place. It's a pretty simple command to teach your dog. Prepare for training, before you tell it to go to its spot, your dog will know how to lie down upon orders. Spend several training sessions focusing on "down." You're able to move on to the position order until your dog can consistently lie down at the order. First, when you send the position order determine where you want your dog to go to. It fits well with a bed or area rug. If you want to be able to use the command in any space, you can easily switch from room to room using a portable bed or matt. When you intend on using clicker training, you'll also need a couple of rewards and a clicker. Pick a button; choose a word to use for orders. Using a single word seems best to work. "Location" is sometimes used but "bed" or "mat" often function well. Lure Your Dog, Begin by standing next to the bed or mat that will serve as the place for your dog. Offer the "location" signal, and then use a reward to attract the dog to their position. If you've got all four paws on the ground, compliment your dog or click the clicker and give it a treat. Repeat the several times. After a few short training sessions, most dogs will go to bed or mate on order. Attach the Down, start telling your dog to lie down until you place all four feet on the mat or bed when you give the order. Give the "place" command, and as soon as the dog gets to the mat, give the "down" command. It might take a few minutes to comply with the first few occasions, but after a few practice sessions, the dog will immediately lie down after you give the "place" command when it reaches the mat. When the dog has done this many times, after you send the "location" order, it will only be getting rewards and praise while it is lying down. Increase the time; now that after you give the "location" order, your dog is regularly lying on its bed, you can increase the amount of time it spends there. To do this, add a few seconds slowly before offering the treat after it answers to the order. When you see improvement, add more small amounts of time gradually.

Your dog is making a mistake and gets up from his position before you give it the treat, give the "location" command again and return to the last point where your dog has been good. By adding gradually to the amount of time your dog is staying in its place, you will be able to send the order quickly and make it stay in its place while you go through whatever you were doing. Switch to Other Rooms, Wait until your dog has learned the command in one place if you want to be able to use the "location" command in other rooms. Move the bed or mat into another room at that point, and start the cycle again. And if you choose not to move the bed from room to room, find a spot in each room that will act as a spot for your dog when providing the "location" order. Many dogs catch on quickly, and when you give the command in a new room, they will automatically go into their bed or mat and lie down. Many dogs will need to know that a new room assumes the same behavior, almost as though you haven't operated on it at all. If that's the case with your dog, start right from the start. Give the signal, draw the dog to the mat and teach it to lie down just as you did in the room before. Wait again until your dog knows the "location" command in the new room before going to the next room. Problems and action proofing, most dogs learn this command relatively quickly. You should have a puppy, with only a few short training sessions, that finds his bed or mat on line. Not being consistent is one of the most common mistakes dog owners make. Dogs tend to hang out in the kitchen, for example, while someone is cooking. Although getting a dog under your feet can be annoying, even dangerous, it's also easy to ignore it, and keep preparing your food. No matter how busy you are, instilling this order into your dog should be your priority— it won't take as long as you think, either. At first it can lead to distractions, but keep in mind the end goal: your dog immediately obeys the command and when told to do so, goes to its location. Today, a little extra time would save you a lot of disappointment in the future.

How to train your dog, to drop something?

- Order "drop it" is utilized to stop the dog from taking stuff. This helps you to warn the dog to not touch anything you aren't allow to have, such as a dirty tissue, kid's toy or many items dogs want to take and bite. This will also discourage the dog from having anything which may be dangerous. Luckily, this essential command can be learned relatively easily. Mostly dogs may be conditioned to "leave behind" only the most wanted items. Prepare yourself; all you have to do is a couple of bite able tidbits and a silent place to teach your dog to "leave it." If you're teaching clickers, you should have the clicker, too.
- This not takes much time to think about? Learning sessions could be kept upbeat and shorter; this is enough for around five mins each time. When your learning sessions are getting to lengthy, your dog could get irritated and begin making mistakes.
- Give Order and Show Tidbits: to begin pick one of the tidbits in the hand and let your dog watch it. Give the order "drop it" and soon it takes interest in the tidbit. Seal your hand so the dog can't get the tidbit.

- First, in an effort to get to the tidbit, most dogs would put their nose in your own hand, and probably nip on your paw or fingers. Offer reward (or clicking) and give it a tidbit and soon the dog stop doing it and get away a bit. The reward you offer your dog is meant to be another reward than one you asked her than take.

- It is very essential that whenever you're in starting stages of learning this order, you keep the treat covered at all times. When you unintentionally let dog to get a reward before you praise or click, so next time it will be really tough to get the reward. Some mistakes won't make barely a difference. But, in case your dog gets the reward a barely any times amid each learning session, it will take them a lot longer to realize what it means to "give it up." Increase Wait Time, when your dog's getting away from your own hand regularly, you might make it easier by many the time you let it stay for the reward. In the starting, the moment it gets back from your hand you will give the dog a tidbit. You can add a couple of moments slowly before you can go for several minutes as your dog stay patiently for the reward. Escalate the Gap; you can start moving your treat next. Place it some feet away from the dog on the floor but hold your hand near enough to mask it if your dog tries to grab it. When your dog has left the tidbit there regularly, you can push it nearer to them a little. Move away, you can start by stepping away from the tidbit yourself after many training sessions. A nice way to start this is by dropping a tidbit onto the floor when you are standing, and giving the order "drop it." Have your foot on alert to cover the reward should your dog leap for it. Raising the gap from the treat steadily through many training meetings. Soon when you are standing on the other side of the house, you will be capable of telling the dog to drop a tidbit on the floor. Practice with Some

Other Things, you can begin playing with other things until your dog has grasped "drop it" with tidbits. Place a dog's toys close it, and say "drop it." Give it reward and a tidbit when the dog gets off a little bit.

- To play with certain things which your dog also enjoys. Your dog would be able to quickly understand to drop every object when he listens the "drop it" signal. Proofing Attitude and Problems this order of compliance is totally about the training self-control to your dog. It's a little bit hard for dogs, after all, to avoid some things, well many things that are both right and wrong to them. You may find it helpful to learn a
  several pronged ways to truly instilling this degree of discipline. When practicing the command "leaves it," make a mark of doing some other things to do self-control exercise. There are easy things like getting your dog to need for meal, affection or playtime by first making them lie or sit down. It can help build this positive behavior in your dog by integrating those things in your everyday activities and having small meetings on drop it every day.

How to train your dog to stay focus on you?
- Significant part of the training of dog is being able to get the dog's entire focus. The "look" and "watch me" order helps to get the dog to concentrate on you. It's useful for occasions when you want to pay careful attention to your pet, for instance during

compliance training. It may also be used when focusing on behavioral issues or when distracting a dog's concentration from items that cause threatening or offensive behaviors. This order is of particular benefit to those who often work with these dogs like a team. For example, people participating in dog compliance or rescue and search could use the order to seek attention from their dog and give them training about what to do now. "Watch me" is a very easy order to say, it doesn't matter what are your demand for it. Get Prepared To train the dog "watch me" order, you'll need some delicious exercise treatments. You'll also want your clicking device on hand while you're working on the clicker exercise. Training "watch me" or "look" is a perfect way if you haven't already done so, to teach the dog clicking therapy.

- Very little to distract your dog, it's very good to start training to order in a place. Select a space inside the home where family members do not bother you. You may also need to do so at a moment meanwhile the home is usually quiet and no distractions are noises like doors or footsteps.
- Name and Order, say your dog's name pursue by the order "look" or "see me" once you've got your clicker and reward ready. For several dogs, listening to their name would be plenty to have their attention. When after you give the order, when dog see your face, you may click or praise on it and then give it a reward. Push the Reward, many dogs

cannot reflex to listening instantly the "watch me" and "look" ordering combined with their name. In this scenario, show a tidbit in front of the dog's nose after you give the order, and then bring the reward up to your face. Your dog is going to follow the reward and then end up staring to your face. Offer the click or praise, and instantly feed the dog a tidbit.

- Will have no trouble having the dog to concentrate its focus on you within a few short training sessions.

- Proofing Attitude and Problems; Often dogs can be easily confused so teaching this order in different of

circumstances is very necessary. To show the actions, continue to practice and slowly step up to work in more noisy surroundings. For example, when your family is very busy go to the identical isolated room during a nosier and busier and time of the day. If your dog's reacting well, switch to another area that's getting more noise and traffic.

- Whenever the dog grasps "watch me" with no disturbances in the house setting, switch into a little alive area, like your backyard. When your dog keeps learning to see you with minimal interference, move to more crowded areas, like other public location. Make sure to educate different people and dogs about the signal. Keep practicing on all these and in any situation you'll soon be capable to have your dog's attention.

How to train your dog to stand up, without moving?

- Very helpful to teach your dog to "stand up" on orders. A simple command is used to tell the dog to stand up without shifting on all four feet. It's helpful to stand up to be checked or groomed anytime you need your dog, whether it's by you or anyone else. This is also a strong base for advanced instruction in compliance. And, if you're planning to show your dog, it's critical because many competitions require a dog to stand still perfectly amid distractions. Fortunately, this is a relatively easy teaching command and most dogs pick it up very quickly.
- "Sit" and "Down," it is important to let your dog learn the commands to sit and down before you teach your dog to stand on order. And if you are still working on those, it's good practice to incorporate stands and can help improve the other order. Prepare for class, what you need is a couple of tidbits to show your dog how to stand. When you are practicing with a clicker, you will still need the clicker. You'll probably want to find a quiet spot free of distractions so your dog remains focused on

you. Introduce "Up," continue sitting or lying in front of you, with your dog. Keep a treat right in front of your nose, and give the "stand" order. Move the treat straight out from your nose and towards you very slowly. The dog will be up for the treat. The moment your dog stands up, thank your dog or click on your clicker to give it the treat. Practice the Order, any time your dog stands up, even if it moves a little, you will reward and treat the first few times you exercise the stand order. When the dog has the feel of it, only when it stands up immediately without moving away from the spot can you begin to give tidbits. After few short training sessions you will be in a position to perfect the stand order.

- Distance and Time, if your dog doesn't travel consistently, increasing the time between you and the dog. Start by taking only one step back after your dog stands and praise your dog for not coming to you. Continue to through the gap before you can take a few steps back away.

- May also stretch the length of your dog's standing without moving at the same time. Start pausing for a few extra seconds, and then wait a full minute, for thirty seconds and then longer before offering a treat. It is a perfect way to instill in your dog self-control, which is the foundation of perfect compliance training.

- And proofing behavior, if you have trouble getting your dog to stand up, you can entice him by providing more reinforcement. There are two effective ways of speaking in an enthusiastic voice or tossing a toy in front of a child. Make sure your dog's stand training start location varies. For e.g., if you started sitting with your dog, exercise the stand command from position down. It should help the dog realize that standing doesn't always apply to sitting. Hold short training sessions, and make sure to stop before your dog loses interest. This is especially important for young puppies, which have a short span of attention and may become irritated or bored after just five minutes. End each session on a positive note, even if you have to go back to a command your dog knows like sitting very well. Prove this activity by putting it into effect in situations where threats occur. Start with your backyard, and then try it out at a public park. Your dog will be paying attention to you in every situation and not what's happening around it. Since groomers and vets may also need your dog to stand up properly, it's nice to get other people around to practice this order. Ask a friend or family member for a few minutes to work with your dog but show them how you do it first. He or she will be able to follow your lead this way, which will make your dog realize that this other person is doing the same thing and they know what to do with it. Send the stand command at your next appointment and your vet or groomer will be impressed with the workout.

How to train your dog to Beg?
- Is a sweet dog trick which is relatively easy for a dog to learn? If you don't like the concept of "begging," you might think of this as "sitting pretty" training your dog, or sitting on the ground with their hind legs and their front paws up in the air. Your dog will soon be sitting up to beg on order with a little patience on your part. All you need is a bit of quiet time and patience. Be sure your dog isn't upset,

has been eating lately and going to the toilet. Get a couple of your dog's favorite tidbits ready to beg before you start practicing. When you are practicing with a clicker, do have your clicker ready. Fast Method to Teach Begging, You're going to start teaching a dog to do this trick by telling them to sit down. When your dog can't sit on order, then go back and focus on the sit order before asking it to beg. When your dog is in a position to sit on order, continue with the instruction. Hold a delight on his nose with your dog in a sitting position and give your pooch the "beg" sign. When your dog tries to take the delight in his mouth, lift the delight above his head slowly so that your dog will have to reach up to get it. Push it up until the dog lies with the front paws off the floor at its hind end and stays in the begging position in front. Say "ok" to your dog or click your clicker and give it a treat as soon as your dog is in the betting place. Follow these measures for brief training sessions, many times a day. It won't be long before your dog begs at the order. Teach Begging in Steps, during the very first training session, some dogs won't be going into the begging place. You may need to teach a dog to beg in smaller steps in this situation. This form of preparation is called shaping. The clicker can be very useful to form behavior. Start with your dog sitting, keep a treat in front of your dog's nose, and give the dog the "beg" order. Push the treat up slowly so your dog will need to raise their nose in the air to reach it. As soon as your dog raises its nose in the air, either click on your clicker or say "ok" to it and give it a treat.

- This process several times until each time you give the beg order, your dog lifts his nose in the air.

- The bar a little higher then. Only click and treat when the nose goes in the air, and one of the paws falls off the ground slightly. Repeat this until every time you give the beg command the dog does it consistently.

- Picking behaviors that get your dog closer to getting into the role of begging. Practice every new action until each time you give the begging order, your dog does so. You'll teach your dog slowly to sit up and beg in this way. If your dog has successfully sat down to beg several times in a row, you can only click and reward when your dog gets on the command to that position. Practice the beg order several times a day for a few minutes. Problems and proofing behavior: If your dog makes a mistake at any point of the training phase more than two or three times in a row, go back to an earlier move. Practice the move until your dog does it correctly at all times, and then start going slowly forward again in training. If your dog has the beg command down, keep practicing and improving it. When you don't remain positive, your dog can miss its exercise. When that happens, then just resume the training again.

How Do You Teach the Dog for A Bow?
- You ever watched a dog doing a bow on signal? It's kind of cute. Dogs love tricks as they are getting most good attention. In case you are able to train it

for sitting and standing, you could simply teach your dog to do a bow on order.

- Dog bends forward with "elbows" to do a bow and its chest hits the floor whilst its rear end remains up. and this is the ideal finish touch when all of your dog's skills are showing off.
- You need is your own the dog as well as some tidbits to teach a dog to take a bow. If you're utilizing a clicking training as piece of your training of dog you may also want to have a clicker on hand. Stand up beginning, and continue to stand up on the all 4 feet for your dog. It's good to make the dog stand up on orders. If this basic order has not yet been mastered, then you might need to work on it prior to moving on to the stage two. Using of Reward to Lower the Dog; place a tidbit at the edge of the dog's nose and push it down slowly, keeping it tight to the body of dog. In this approach, you'll use the reward to coax the dog lower till its paws are onto the floor and its hindquarters are left high. Turning Back to Standing, keep the dog in a bow position for a couple of moments after that use the reward to encourage him back to standing. Bow Rewarding, say "good" or "yeah" or do clicking and feed the tidbit to dog as soon as your dog finishes the bow and is standing up. Repeat that many times. Include an Order Word; you should include the signal word "bow" prior going through steps two and three again, until your dog appears to understand the action. Rehearse the bow ordering for your own dog for no longer than five mins per day, several times a day. The dog will do the bow on order, before you know it. Trick breaking in stages, some of the dogs are having a hard time getting this

entire skill at the moment. In this case for the dog, in lesser amounts, you should train it to do a bow. This is known as behavior shaping, and the clicking training works well too. You have to start praising the dog for going in the correct direction to do so. For example, in case the best trick the dog can do before doing wrong is to get the reward halfway up to the ground, reward and click for that. So only start offering tidbits when your dog is closer to the floor. So, you can pick actions that come nearest to what the dog wants to do. You should slowly teach your dog to do a bow, in small steps over many training sessions. Proofing Attitude and Problems, for you and the dog it takes time to teach the dog to get some new trick. When your dog starts to lose focus in your exercise session. Please never kick or scream at your dog as you attempt to teach them during new trick. Just your pet would get confused. Keep in mind to be careful when exercising with your dog and yourself. Each dog learns differently. Keep short and optimistic training sessions, and make sure to finish on a good note. It can mean ordering the dog that it knows very well and ends up providing exuberant reward and praise. Many dogs have difficulty balancing their backside in air after getting this trick at first. Put your hand under the stomach of the dog while using other hand to coax its front side to the ground to hold its back half up while its chest and elbows are resting on the floor Some dogs will catch on easily, particularly if they already know some other skills, and the dog will do the bow after a few rehearsing sessions without you keeping its back. If the dog does it in any setting, you'll know the trick is "proofed." Ultimately, try training the dog to plea for a new trick.

How to train your Dog to Spin?

- Your dog, old or young, with a new trick of doing a command twirl. You can teach a dog to only turn in one direction or you can teach your pet to differentiate between right and wrong. Either way, just a couple of tidbits are all you need to teach a dog to spin. When you're teaching clickers, you should have a clicker on hand as well. Teach a Simple Spin, you'll want to start with your dog in a standing position to teach your dog how to spin. When your dog doesn't know how to stand on orders, doing it first would be faster, and then focusing on spinning. You are ready to get started with a couple of tidbits in your pocket. Give your dog a treat in front of his face. Slowly drag the treat towards the side of your dog's mouth, and to obey the treat, it has to turn its mouth.
- Moving the treat all the way around your dog's body in a circle and it'll need to spin to keep track of the treat.
- Your dog has completed the reward in a full circle, say "yes" or "no" to the pup or click on the clicker. Then give your dog a fast treat. Repeat several times on steps 2 and 3. When your dog appears to understand the action, add the word "spin" command before repeating steps 2 and 3 again. Spend several times a day performing the spin for about five minutes. Before you know it, the dog can turn around in a full circle. Attach Direction; you can start teaching your canine to learn directions once the dog twirls on an order. Start with a treat

right in front of your dog's nose as you did above. Adjust the order this time to "right spin" or "left spin." Give the instruction, and pull your dog's treat in the direction you want it to spin. Each day, engage in a few brief training sessions. Make sure you only focus on one new command (right or left spin) at a time before your dog knows the difference between the two commands. When your dog knows how to turn both left and right on order, you can start mixing it up. In one training session, ask it to spin in various directions. When your dog is able to respond correctly to the command consistently by turning in the right direction, you will know it has a clear understanding of the difference between the two commands. Problems and proofing behavior while in only a few training sessions some dogs may learn to spin, others can get stuck or find it difficult to complete a spin. Others may experience difficulty learning to spin the first time in a full circle. You can start smaller in this case, and work up to spin all the way around. This technique is called forming, and the clicker works outstandingly well.

- By pulling a treat to one side of your dog's head, if you need to shape the spinning action. Click or say "ok" to the dog as soon as it turns its head, and offer a treat. When it's turning its head regularly, you should start clicking and rewarding only when the dog turns its head and takes a step to turn around. In this way, you will gradually pick the behaviors that will get your dog closer to turning around completely until the pet turns in a full circle with only one reward at the end. If it looks like your dog understands the order but then starts making mistakes, chances are you've pushed too quickly forward. In this situation, just go back a few steps to when your dog was thoroughly productive. Practice the move for a few sessions, and then gradually start going forward again. Dogs will get dizzy much like humans. Training for too long is a common mistake, and may result in a dizzy and confused dog. Just exercise for a short period of time and if your dog just appears to hate the training or the feeling of spinning, there is no need to proceed. There's no particular sense in a twirl dog command and it's just a fun trick so if your dog can't do it, think on other stuff your dog does well.

How to train your Dog to shake paws?
- Dog and a couple of tidbits are the only things needed when teaching a dog to shake paws. When you're practicing for clickers, you'll need your clicker too. This trick relies calmly on the dog sitting and giving you its indivisible attention. If it doesn't know how to sit consistently, before going on, go back and practice the order.
- "Shake" Let the dog lie down. Keep in one hand a treat, and give it to your dog. Place your hand over the treat so the dog will not be able to get it.
- Your dog the "shake" signs, and waves your closed fist under her nose to keep her involved in the treat. Wait for your dog to begin searching for the reward into your pocket. Normally dogs are sniffing around, and when that doesn't work they start pawing on your side. The moment your dog puts his paw on your palm, says "ok" or clicks on your clicker. Open your hand and let the dog have the treat.

- "Shakes" for five minutes, two or three times a day. Your dog can offer you his paw as soon as you give the order before you know it. Once your dog offers his paw on request, you will start phasing out the need to keep the treat in your closed hand. Begin the treat with your hand closed and give your dog the "shake" command.

How to train your dog to wave on cue?
- Your dog how to wave is a simple dog trick that will thrill everyone and impress them. However, teaching a dog to raise his paw and wave hello or goodbye isn't all that difficult either. Your dog and some yummy dog tidbits are everything you need. When you use the clicker instruction, the clicker will be handy too. The Treat Process, first it should know how to shake paws before you start teaching a dog to wave. Waving is created from what the dog knows when it's shaking your hand. When your dog has not yet learned to shake, the best thing to do is to go back and practice on that skill. Then, you can start teaching the wave when you are ready. Give your dog the order, "shake." After raising your paw to shake your hand, raise your hand up slightly, so you have to raise the paw up a little to get your hand on. Click on your clicker or say "no," or "yes," and give the dog a treat when your dog pushes the paw faster than it can go to shake it.
- It many times. Each time you lift your hand up a little higher until your dog lifts the paw above your head. If your dog has put his paw several times in a row, give the "shake" command. If your dog begins to touch the paw, give the "wave" command (or use the "say hello" or "wave bye" command) and follow

steps two to four again. Repeat this many times, before the dog lifts its paw regularly. Stop using the shake command after a number of repetitions, and just give the "wave" command. Many dogs soon learn to lift their paw on order above their head. You can be more selective and search for the best waves until your dog's doing it reliably on orders. Start offering tidbits only when the hand is over the head and go up and down a little in a wave motion. The Clicker Method, You can be able to teach them to wave by catching the gesture if you use a clicker to train your dog. Many dogs use their paws to get your attention and with your clicker you can catch this action and use it to teach your dog how to wave. Keep your clicker and some medications handy, and then click on your clicker and give it a treat the next time your dog paws at you. Do this many times, to get your attention every time your dog lifts its paw. A dog that's used to using clickers will soon start giving activities to try and get a reward. Continue to click and offer tidbits any time the hand is lifted.

- Add the "shock" button. Say the order, and wait. Click and treat every time your dog raises its head. Your dog will soon be offering the action faster after you have issued the order. When your dog is waving on order regularly, you will start clicking and rewarding for the movements that look like a wave the most. Problems and proofing behavior, Keep short and upbeat training sessions. Practice the wave command at a time, two or three times every day, for a few minutes. Be careful and note both dogs are thinking a little differently. When your dog is bored or irritated, wrap up the session and then try again. Seek always to finish on a good note, such as looking at a simple order like sit or down. Dogs are easily confused so it's a good idea to show the action if you want yours to pull this trick off in front of people. When your dog knows about it in the home, go out to the yard where a few more distractions will be available. And in a park or in another public spot, you may do the same. You can also practice in the room with someone in your house and if a guest comes through the door. Your dog would easily impress all your friends after a little practice, as it greets them with a wave!

How to Train the Dog to Give You Kisses?
- Several people, particularly children, give kisses on order are a beloved dog skill. It also appears to be the simplest tricks a dog can be taught to do. Any tasty tidbits are all you want to be teaching this simple skill. Cream cheese or Peanut butter works great, as it's really easy to stain your hand or cheek a little bit. Also, you may want to have a towel at present, particularly if you're dealing with the dog well-known to be a drooled, such as Mastiff or St. Bernard. You will need a ready human being participant who's frank to the dog slobber concept on their nose. Train a Dog to give Kiss: now, follow a few simple stages to train the sweet skill to your dog. Be careful to have this method handy for your tidbit. Take some cream cheese or peanut butter, and put some on your face (or kiss your dog anywhere you want). Also, you can ask something such as "gimme sugar" or "give me kisses". Bend towards

the dog, and allow your dog to do the work. The dog will be happy to lick your face with the treat. Rehearse this trick many times a day for some time. You don't have to wait; your dog comes to give you a kiss whenever you order him. Another way to teach a dog to give you kisses is to catch the action with a reward or Clicker. When your dog is licking you, order to "give you kisses". You may also utilize a Clicker to set the action; just start clicking anytime you kiss your dog. Say "nice" to the puppy when your dog has given a hug to you, and give it a tidbit. The dog would soon receive instruction to give kisses on order, and all you had to grab the normal habits of the dog. Proofing Attitude and Problems, some dogs are a little too vigorous, and when you train them to give a kiss it may be hard to get dogs to stop. You can bring a stop to these kisses on order in this situation, too. Whenever your dog kisses you, say "enough" to the pup. Hold till your dog finish licking you, then say "ok" to the dog and offer a treat to your pup. Do this whenever your dog gives you a lot of kisses, and you should order the dog to end licking you if the kissing gets out of hand early. Some dogs stop giving kisses on your faces to people. If that's the case with your own dog, you may try using a tidbit it really likes or you may teach the dog to give a kiss on other places, like on your face. Using the same stages as above but place the tidbit on the back side of your hand instead of your nose. One approach for some people to train their dog to give a kiss is to place a gourmet treat on the human face like a biscuit, and allow the dog to have it from here. This isn't suggested for several reasons. You wouldn't want to exchange germs too closely, and promoting them isn't a reasonable (or healthy) practice. It's also a bad practice of allowing children to see dog therapies as something people place in their mouths. It gives out the bad message to children and may be frustrating. Keep in your mind that while you might like your dog's wet sloppy and big kisses, not everyone appreciates the attention. In case you're practicing this dog skill on visiting kids or your friends, you might like to train your dog to give some kisses on hands instead on cheek. You'll also need to be sure the person leans down and accepts the dog's kiss at the stage. You wouldn't want your dog to reach up or get up to offer the kisses. Normally this isn't a welcoming attitude, and it might scare (knock down) kids, particularly if you are having a big dog.

Chapter 3: Box and Clicker Training for Dogs

In this chapter, we will learn about the different type of training for our dogs, also known as box training and clicker training, these are considered traditional methods of training your pets particularly dogs, the entire chapter will cover a best guide for advanced training of dog as well as traditional use of house training.

3.1 Box Training

Box teaching harnesses the innate instincts of your dog as an animal of shelter. Their house is a wild dog's den-a place to sleep, hide from danger, and raise a family. The box is the den of your dog, where they can find warmth and isolation while you know that they're protected and comfortable (and not shredding your house while you're on the run). The main use of a box is housetraining, as dogs do not like soiling their dens. The box will restrict access to the rest of the house while learning other rules, including not chewing on furniture. Boxes are a convenient way to hold the dog inside the vehicle too.
Crating cautions:
A box is not a perfect solution to typical canine behavior. Any dog can feel stuck and irritated if not used correctly. Always using the box as punishment. Your dog would get afraid of it and refuse to enter. Don't lock your dog for too long in the box. A dog that is boxd all day and night is not having enough exercise or human contact, and can become depressed or nervous. You will need to change your routine, hire a pet sitter or send your dog to a daycare center to cut down on the amount of time they spend each day in their box.

Puppies under the age of six months should not be left in a box for more than three to four hours at a time. After so long they cannot regulate their bladders and intestines. The same goes with housetraining adult dogs. Physically, it can be kept by an elderly dog but they don't feel they can. Only shred your dog before you can trust them not to wreck the house. Thereafter, it should be a place they happily go. Your dog's den might be a cage, but just as you wouldn't spend your entire life in one room in your house, your dog shouldn't spend much of their time in their cage. Can you imagine your dog living in a cage for years? Support us to stop chicken mills.

Process of Training

This type of training may take few days till weeks, it depends on age, past experience and temperament of your dog. When training it is important to keep two things in mind: Box can always be attached with some nice things and training could be done in a sequence of small steps. Don't get started too quickly.

First Step: Box Introduction to The Dog

Put the box in a place of your home where all the family put a great deal of time, like the room for whole family sitting. Put a warm towel or blanket inside the box. Remove off the door and let the dog play at leisure on the box. Many dogs may be naturally curious, and instantly continue to sleep in the box. If yours isn't one of them, take them to the box and speak to with them in a positive voice tone. Be sure the door to the box is open and locked so it won't reach the dog and scare them. Encourage your dog to reach the box by dropping nearby some small dog meal tidbits, then just into the door, and eventually, into the box totally. If at first, they hesitate to go fully inside the box, that's OK; don't trick them into going in. Continue to throw tidbit inside the box before the dog movers quietly through the box to get the food. Try throwing a pet toy in the box in case they aren't involved in tidbits. It can take a couple of mins to many days.

Second Step: Feed the Meals in Box

Start feeding them their daily meals inside the box, after adding your dog to the box. It will build an enjoyable bond with the box. When your dog enters the box readily when you start Step 2, put the food bowl at the back of the box all the way. When they remain hesitant to enter, only bring the dish inside until they are able to go without being nervous or afraid. Every time you give them meal, place the plate back in the box a little more. When your dog is safely standing in the box to consume their food, you should shut the door when they are consuming food. The first time you do that, when they finish their meal, open the door. You should keep the door shut for a few minutes longer for each successive feeding, before they remain in the box for about 10 minutes after eating. When they start whining to be let out, you might have been too fast to raise the amount of time. Next time seek to abandon them in the box for a short duration of time. Do not allow the dog to get out before they rest, if they do complain or scream in the box. Perhaps they will know the moaning is the way to get out of the box and they can continue to do it.

Third Step: Practice with Longer Boxing Duration

Since eating your dog's daily meals in the box without any sign of discomfort or fear, you should leave them there for brief periods of time when you're at home. Call them up to the box and reward them with a reward. Give them an entrance order, like "kennel." Encourage them by pointing a treat in your hand to the inner side of the box. After dog reach to the box you should admire them, feed them the treat, and shut the door. Sit quietly by the box for 5 to 10 mins, and after that go to other room for a couple of minutes. Return, sit back quietly for a brief time, and then allow them to out of the box. Repeat this cycle several times a day, growing slowly the length of time you abandon them in the box and the length of time you're out of reach. When your dog sits comfortably in the box with you mostly away from eyes for around 30 minutes, you will continue to leave them boxed while you are out for short periods of time and may or may not let them sleep there at nightfall. This can take days or weeks to complete.

Fourth Step: Box the Dog While You Leaving

When the dog is free to spend about 30 minutes in the box without being nervous or scared, when you leave the house you will continue to leave them boxed for short durations. Using your usual command and a reward to bring them inside the box. You may want to leave them in the box with a few healthy toys too. Vary the moment you put the dog in the box while you are getting ready to go routine. Even if they shouldn't be boxed long before you leave, you should box them anyplace from 5 to 20 mins early before going. Don't emotionally and prolong your departure, they should be matter-of-fact. Briefly thank your dog, feed them a reward for running into the box, and after that go quietly. Should not feed the dog for some nice activity when you get home, by listening enthusiastically to them. Hold low noise arrivals to prevent growing anxiety when you come back. Keep in mind to box your dog when you're at home for brief duration of time, because they don't equate boxing with being abandoned alone. Using your usual order and a reward to put your dog inside the box. First, placing the box in your sleeping room or in a hallway nearby may be a good idea, particularly if you have a canid. Puppies also have to go out to shed during the night and you're going to want to be capable of listening to your dog as they cry to be let out. Initially, Elder dogs should be kept nearby too, because they don't equate the box with isolation socially. When your dog sleeps peacefully through the night with the box near you, you can start transferring it slowly to the position you prefer, while time spent with your dog— even sleeping time — is an opportunity to deepen the connection between you and your pet. When your dog sleeps comfortably with his box near you through the night, you can start moving it slowly to the location you prefer, while time spent with your dog— even sleeping time — is an opportunity to reinforce the connection between you and your pet. Potential problems... Moaning. If the dog whines or cries at night when in the box, it might be difficult to determine whether they are moaning to get out of the box, or whether they need to be let out to remove. Unless you have understood the training, protocols mentioned above, so in the past the dog was not punished for crying by being released from their box. If that is the case, then begin avoiding the moaning. When your dog is just checking you, they are likely to stop crying very soon. Yelling or banging at them on the box would only make it worse. When the moaning persists after several minutes of ignoring them, use the word they equate with going outside to remove them. If they get excited and react, take them outside. This should be a purpose-based outing, not play-time. When you're persuaded you don't have to kill your dog, the safest approach is to neglect them till they stop barking. Don't give in; if you do, you can teach the dog long and loud to scream to get what they desire. When you have gone through the steps of training slowly and haven't achieved too much too soon, you will be less likely to experience the problem. When the situation is unmanageable, the box training cycle can need to start over again. Anxiety over separation. The effort to use the box as a separation anxiety solution does not fix the issue. A box can prevent destruction of your dog but in an effort to escape they may get injured. Problems of separation anxiety may only be addressed by desensitization and counterconditioning procedures. You may want to receive assistance from a licensed animal-behavior specialist. See below for more on separation anxiety.

3.2 Clicker training

Clicker training is similar to positive reinforcement training, with a clicker added value. A clicker is actually a mechanical tiny noisemaker. The strategies are based on animal learning science which states that rewarded behaviors are more likely to be replicated in the future. And instead of concentrating on what your dog is doing wrong, and taking good behavior as a matter of course, clicker training flips the script and focuses on what your dog is doing right. You will have an amazing effect on how your dog wants to behave by asking your dog what to do, instead of what not. The clicker's benefit is it shows your dog precisely what actions you're gratifying over. You can "mark" the moment your dog has done what you wanted, by clicking at the right time. And instead of trying to guess what you've wanted; the click shows your dog exactly what they did right. For example, if you are teaching your dog to sit down, at the moment your dog's butt hits the ground, you can click on it.

What is the meaning of click and how does it help?

The clicker is nothing more than a way to mark a moment. There's nothing special about the specific noise and you will never make it outside of training with your dog. And, as long as it's different from other ways you interact with your dog, you can use something as a marker. You might snap your fingers, blow a whistle or clutch your tongue, for example. Many people use a marker word such as "yes" or "nice." You can use a light or a soft tap on the shoulder for a hearing impaired dog. The click or other symbol itself would of course be meaningless before it is combined with a reward. The click indicates clearly that a reward is on the way. While the best motivation for most dogs is tasty tidbits, a reward is all your dog values are. So if your dog wants to fight for a tug-of-war game rather than a piece of chicken, play this instead. Timing and continuity are essential components. The click must mark the correct moment, followed by a reward for every button. How Does Clicker Training Help?

After performing a desirable behavior a dog is rewarded in positive reinforcement training. Without using a clicker or any other marker, what's being rewarded could be clear to the trainer, but is it obvious to the dog? When you teach a dog to lie down, for instance, how do you make it clear that you are rewarding the belly on the ground? You have to make sure that the reward is given while the dog lies down and not the dog gets up to get it. Otherwise, the dog may think the reward would be to stand up or walk towards you. With food treatments that's easy, but impossible if the reward is a round of fetching or tugging. What about dogs those pop up when they touch the floor from a down? You may not get them the reward fast enough. Or, what about more challenging behaviors such as those performed remotely? How do you get a reward from your dog for jumping through a hoop at the precise moment they cross the line? That's where the click power or some other marker comes in. The click marks the moment you will be rewarded, then bridges the gap in time until the reward comes. Your dog knew exactly what was right in practice. But you just couldn't use the same sort of praise? You could, but that isn't nearly as obvious. You interact with your dog all the time using praise. It's a great part of genuinely praising your puppy. Plus, there is nothing unique to the training situation about recognition, nor would you want that to be the case. Gushing over your dog is part of the joy of owning a dog. Using a clicker or other training-specific symbol eliminates uncertainty about the coming reward. Clicker-trained dogs tend to enjoy knowing, in addition to the value of understanding. They want to practice to earn a click and work hard. Mark and award training, from your dog's point of view, makes teaching new behaviors a game. This also takes the trainer off pressure. Looking for clickable moment's means concentrating on the positive decisions your dog has made, rather than dwelling on errors. Clicker training, like any form of positive reinforcement training, enhances your communication, strengthens your relationship with your dog, and makes the training enjoyable.

How Do You Use Clicker Training?

You would first need to show the dog what the marker means to use a clicker or some other marker. Also called "loading the clicker," you paired a reward with your chosen marker. So, just press, and then treat immediately. The dog should realize, after about 10–20 repetitions, that the symbol signals a reward to come. You are now able to bring this clicker into action. For the attract-and-reward technique, you can use your marker, where you use a reward to encourage your dog into the action you are after. But it's also important to mold behaviors. By baby steps, shaping includes developing a complex behavior. The clicker is a perfect means of identifying positive actions, too. And if you see your dog lying peacefully on a mat rather than begging at the table, then press reward the behavior. And if, when the doorbell rings, your dog has all four paws on the floor, press the moment before your dog has a chance to leap on visitors. Last but not least, the practicing of clickers is a perfect way to teach tricks. Finally, you do no longer need the symbol because your dog has mastered a new behavior. It is just a teaching tool, after all. But the clicker or other marker will help you interact clearly with your dog if you want to attract, form or catch an action, so the action you want is the behavior you'll get.

Procedure:

In clicker coaching is one growing method of constructive strengthening. This quick and efficient form of training uses a clicker, that is a metallic strip within a tiny plastic container that when pushed creates a distinctive clicking tone. The clicking is much quicker and further distinctive than saying "nice dog" and far more successful than only treat-only teaching. A reward is offered shortly after clicking, to show a dog the purpose of the click. When the dog knows about the click sound's beneficial impact, the clicker on its own serves as a programmed motivator. Clickers may be sold in most big pet shops, and they are fairly affordable.

You can teach the dog to answer the clicker with ease. Then you can move on into simple and high-level training. The use of a stepwise technique of training is also indicate as clicker preparing.

Bind Clicker Training to Prize, this training isn't intended to take over the usage of tidbits entirely. The clicking sound immediately tells your dog that it will earn a reward for what it has done. To reinforce this, tidbits will always accompany clicks. The clicker would otherwise drop its capability. "When some of the clicker instructor do not reward each time they push click button, with a reward, almost all clicker instructor tend to pursue the clicking," instructor Alyssa Walker. "The use of strong rewards during early training periods is very significant, and corrections are also the best incentive for the dog." Also, the foundation for training of clicker rests in the operant process, a psychological concept that explains how animals understand from the effects of such attitude. Constructive strengthening is a type of operant process which is mostly used in training of dog. If you're going to deliver many of tidbits, consider using small (yet still appealing) tidbits that a dog love. Using small portions of unseasoned baked chicken or turkey for a simple, low-cost alternative during your workout. Begin a Quiet Environment; leave the dog in a peaceful environment with no distractions. Ideally, you should do this exercise while the dog is tired. Get a couple of the best tidbits ready for your dog and inside your pocket the clicker. Activate the Mouse, and then press the mouse. Feed your dog a tidbit right away after pressing the clicker. Do this variation of click / treat five to ten times. Check the dog, if your dog does not pay attention to you, you can check your performance by tapping. Whenever your own dog immediately looks at you and answers the click, then you are able to go on looking for a tidbit. If not, start the mix of click-treat till the dog knows each clicking means a tidbit. Using the clicking device to teach the dog simple commands. Push the button at the precise moment that your dog is doing the desired action. Start with a tidbit and the praise. When you do not push the click at the exact time, the dog would be puzzled and uncertain as to what reward the treat has received. Some of the clicker's great qualities in this are precision. The dog connects its acts with the clicking and the reward thereafter. The dog not only knows exactly what is it doing, but it also makes the pet more probably to redo the behavior when prompted in the coming time. This training might also be very useful for high level training. "You just click to the behavior for little steps and work on the dog towards the final, finished attitude," says Walker. "This helps you to be indulgent (other than of course, to offer the reward), you may not need to push a dog into place, which can also slow down the procedure." In general, clicker is a really useful device in the exercise. Try using the clicker when developing your dog's compliance and training plan, and see how good the strategy fits for you. Proofing Attitude and Problems, it is common mistake to neglect the strengthening when you use the clicking device for training of dog. Although your own dog has been taught to answer to the clicking, it often follows the actions you take to earn your praise. Don't neglect a dog's owner's need for attention, devotion, and affection. As clicker teaching is based on reward, in case the dog has a low dietary drive or is not driven by treats (or tidbits), this type of training is unlikely to work. Additionally, if you use clicking training for more progressive exercises or movements, you may want a really accurate coordinated control of eye movement with hand movement and full focus to clicking at the same time you want. In case you can't do that, you'll get your dog confused and drive to lousy training.

Clicker Training a Puppy:

A perfect way to train puppies to think, please and teach is a form in training of dog known as clicking based training. Training puppies with clickers is simple. People and puppies will redo attitude that award them, and neglect attitude that do not provide any value. Owners should not be professional dog owners to utilize this strategy and puppies understand how to act very quickly. A puppy finds out of how can he deal with the results are an added benefit. This empowers the canid and persude him to think of ideas to do his bidding by wondering what good behavior you're going to reward. This also encourages your puppy to appreciate and see forward to lessons in training of dog as they become a way and game and for yourself to interact with one another. A dog called Magic learned very easily using the clicker training. By the age of 10 weeks, on local TV station, he did "push-ups of puppy." Your puppy will understand simply as quickly and puppies are in fact sponges ready to learn new things. Allow them a form of spending all the energy constructively.

Clicker Training Introduction

This training allows the act that you want your puppy to do stumble across. Once he mistakenly sits, he'll perform several "incorrect" behaviors and get a prize. The canid finds out that if he may guess as well as show the action that you want, he will receive a reward. The more he tries incorrect habits, the more he knows what is not going to work. In clicker training, you cannot use orders or physical guidance, it's just encouraged dog, and the dog never gets penalty however he's only awarded for the correct option. Now, follow how this works. Rather than trying to find something wrong with your puppy, capture him doing some good thing. Label your activity with a different signal so puppy knows your action (for instance sitting) is what exactly you want. You may utilize a phrase like the YES! And just like a clicking sound. Clicker clearly states he was right to your puppy. Instead he will be rewarded with praise, rewards or a pet. Pick whatever drift the boat of your puppy, and book the most coveted award for these sessions of training.

"Click" Demonstration, to accelerate the procedure, instructors suggest that you should "load" the clicking device so the pet can easily associate the sound of an imminent reward. Here's how you can to do that. Now, fill an empty bowl of smelly treats like Liver bits, bacon, hot dog slices or other highly aromatic morsels do best. It's not about feeding his stomach and upseting his appropriate diet, that's why the treats shouldn't function.

Training puppies and dogs with clicker to stop chasing cats:

Famously, the puppies and kittens being brought up together get along. Even adult pets, if introduced properly, can learn to live with "the weird critter." One of the most common issues, though, includes showing respect for your new puppy and not chasing your cat repeatedly. Some dogs feel obligated to track down cats. Motion causes their inborn predatory instinct for herding and terrier forms to follow. Keys, of course, do not like being made into a wind-up toy for the fun of the dog. The "chase" is, in some instances, life-threateningly dangerous. Luckily, there are a variety of strategies that you can use to teach your puppy to refrain from chasing, promote good behavior and keep kitty safe.

Muzzle for Protection, a muzzle for your puppy may be the best and safest choice in extreme cases where you truly believe the fur would escape. A basket muzzle is an ideal choice to keep the cat secure from a naive puppy. To embrace the muzzle, you'll need to teach your dog: Show the muzzle to the puppy. Let it smell the muzzle so it transforms into a familiar object. Keep the muzzle in the basket like a mug. Within place a favorite treat, and show it to the puppy. Keep the muzzle so that the dog sticks his nose inside to collect the treat. Repeat a dozen times feeding your dog the muzzle gourmet tidbits. Finally, fasten the muzzle and praise the dog for tolerating it with some tidbits. So just take it off. Do not give tidbits unless the muzzle is worn and the dog associates it with tidbits. For dogs that salivate at cat's sight, make sure they wear the muzzle if you can't oversee the pair. Carrier tactics, most dogs don't mean harming the cat; they're just not able to resist the chase lure. Trainers are proposing a few methods that can remedy that. One option is for the cat to use a safe carrier when the puppy is under leash supervision. Just use this strategy if your cat is a relaxed feline and is not going to get unduly nervous. Shy cats should not be put under this circumstance. While the puppy is in another house, that your kitty in a safe carrier. To help keep the cat happy, have a toy or catnip. Bring the puppy into the room and give one after the other her favorite therapies to keep her focused on you and to reward the relaxed behavior. Tell the dog to practice a stay, to follow you in a heel position on the leash or to remain in command. Practice compliance commands that are very well known to your puppy and reward her for obeying. Offer the right incentives for the cat to shift or look away. The aim is to teach your puppy that by avoiding the cat, it gets more treatment and rewards, rather than harass it. "Cookie Cat" technique, "cookie cat" technique works better. Just like Pavlov trained dogs to salivate when they heard a bell, you should train your puppy to respond to the presence of the cat in such a way as to make it difficult to start the chase. Ensure the safety of the cat by keeping the dog under leash control and avoiding any chase.

Chapter 4: Professional training of dogs

In the near future, this chapter will cover the dogs ' professional training section, which will consist of dog services in paramilitary institutes and other specialized departments where they act as a common member. This chapter will cover how to train dogs in a professional manner to help and facilitate professional deployments.

4.1 Training dogs for military standards

Whilst the training your dog that sound overwhelming, and afterwards trying to persuade my dog that it's not really my room, her room, or that she can eat squirrels may not be fluffy chew toys, I know it's also periodically annoying.

However, that needn't be a dispute. Purpose and Task interact with Mike Dowling, an Iraq War Marine veteran and a retired army dog trainer, for some training of dog tips. Dowling also works with Heroes and Hounds, a non-profit organization that offers dogs to army veterans, "You want to create trust in your dog instantly and be optimistic in them," Dowling said, adding that a healthy relationship among dog and its or handler or instructor is an integral cornerstone in the process.

And the reason for that is compliance. "All stems from compliance, because if they don't heal whenever you order them to heel or sit whenever you order them to sit, they're not going to do anything else," Dowling said. "We are equals in a person to person relationship. You are the alpha in a human-to-dog connection and this is vital as they depend on you for guidance and safety." Moreover, Dowling clarified that there is no fixed timetable for your dog's training. "It begins as you sense that the dog count on you along with you've got a sufficient friendship and deep enough bond, they'll follow you, so there's really no timeline for that," Dowling said. "It just depends on your dog and you." When your dog gets on throughout years or has come to you with a range of nasty habits and you're concerned because they are too entrenched, Dowling claims the old saying "old dogs won't learn new skills" is just that, tired and obsolete. "Never mind what age any dog will know," Dowling said. "Just like humans, dogs are constantly learning." While knowing the significance of compliance in training is one thing, putting it into action is something else. When training your dog, you must do 3 things, Dowling explained: Be consistent, optimistic and cautious.

4.2 Police training for dogs

Although dogs work for individuals around the globe in a number of ways, the police dogs are the most popular service dogs. These dogs (K9) manage multiple tasks including guarding the owner of the dog, drugs or explosives sniffing and patrolling vulnerable areas.

Every work involves distinct sets of skills, and so a distinct form of training. Training of police dog (K9) starts while the dog is just a puppy. Many dog breeds like German Shepherds are genetically engineered for security and policing purposes, whilst Bloodhounds and Labradors are generally more skilled for roles like the detection and searching of other products (drugs, bombs,).You have already taken one right step towards good K9 training of dog by picking the best breed and utilizing the skills he inherently contains, Another element to consider while picking a dog to be trained like a police dog is the puppy's temperament. Police dogs have to be calm, alert, intelligent and obedient. They can't be anxious or nervous because, at best, those characteristics would make them barely able to perform and worst side is being dangerous. Training in socialization and compliance is critical once a canid is picked, then proper training in socialization and compliance. When the puppy is growing, those basic fundamental aspects must be strictly in place. The canid has to be capable of sitting, standing, coming and going down on orders while off-leash and on-leash. Constant evaluations and testing, the puppy will be evaluated at

each stage of training to check if it has cleared the test. If he doesn't clear, at that point he won't move into the complete training program. That full coaching course contains an ample range of analysis in various situations. Dogs need to be capable of doing their jobs under heat, in noisy stressful conditions and with little instruction at times. Hence their preparation includes models that are constantly performed again and again. Weapons are shot, fictional bad people begin to run away as if they were trying to flee, doors are smacked and cars screeched, close to scenes you see performed in action films! Keeping funny things, like with any kind of training, K9 training of dog sessions are fashioned as funny as they can, so that the dog will encounter all of this valuable prep work with his occasionally dangerous job as a game. Good exercise prevents the dog from failing his attraction or being burnt out. Champions of scenting, police dogs that are given duties that involve the usage of their specific scenting abilities, like those that need to track criminals or check for explosives or drugs may undergo advanced training to help them identify the items they need to find. For starters, dogs used by DEA should be capable of differentiate between the marijuana smell and the burgers and French fries smell. Bought police dogs, the police departments also purchase dogs that are already qualified. In these situations the first focus of the training should be the association of new proprietor with the dog. The proprietor of the dog must be conditioned to recognize the previously learned knowledge of the dog further the dog should be modified where appropriate and he needs to handle the new owner's orders. Constant preparation, Police Dog Work never ceases. They're practicing all the time when they're not even on patrol so they're always ready for the day whenever their unique talents are required. The dogs usually stay with their instructor and they constantly establish their relationship. Time and again, this relationship and thorough preparation has provided remarkable outcomes whenever a police dog catches a suspect, detects a explosive in a public place, or through his professional abilities and intuitive intelligence saves his partner's life.

4.3 Training of dog programs of military

Breeds of Servicing Dog

A large part of United States army servicing dogs are Dutch and German shepherds as well as breeds of Belgian

Malinois, these dogs are "very combative, very intelligent, very energetic and very faithful." As stated by Rolfe. Moreover, "we demand much more of them they need to be solid and competitive with us" also "we would like a strong-strung dog of violent tendencies, which is what the task requires" stated by him. These dogs are being recognized as "power multipliers" by the world's military armed forces, The Romans rounded their dogs with razor-sharp collars, and sent them into the ranks of the foe to attack and bite their enemies said by Rolfe.

DOD Servicing Dogs History

After the War of independence, the United States army has been using working dogs, first as herd animals, and then for many sophisticated purposes, including killing of rats throughout the ditches in 1st World War, stated by him. Yet 2nd World War saw the largest increase in the utilization of servicing dogs to aid combat operations. Above than ten thousand uniquely trained canids are employed by the United States army, most of them as guards but some as mine detectors, messengers and spies, explained by Rolfe. At present, "a few hundred" servicing dogs operate as surveillance dogs, drug and explosives detectors dogs with United States army in Afghanistan and Iraq, said by Rolfe, moreover contractors are using extra dogs in the theatre. Almost 2000 more servicing dogs are offering similar services around the world at United State operational posts and bases. The army, meanwhile, is growing their dependence on servicing dogs. Rolfe stated the in a year Air Force had trained nearly 200 servicing dogs for DOD prior to Sept. 11, 2001. The figure is over 500 and a lot of dogs are trained as bomb detectors and sentries.

Training Program
The dogs learn fundamental compliance and more advanced techniques, like how to target and sniff out different materials in two-month program. Rolfe stated that the basic training plan of the 341st team of Training Squadron is focused around "good incentives" usually a rubber toy or ball instead of food. "We discovered years ago that dog food only lasts so long. All the dog actually needs is to play with you." After the dogs undergo their basic training, 37th Security Unit members advise the trainers and dogs to do team work. "To get a trainer to know what really a dog exhibits to him is one of the greatest obstacles," Staff Sgt. Sean Luloffs of Air Force, a school teacher said. "But seeing the teams becoming better and capable of competing at an increased level is the major reward, and realizing you've had a role in it," Mier added.

Bringing a Dog to a School:
You will meet our therapy dog, Boomer, as you walk down a hall in my classroom. Initially there were concerns about getting a service dog in our community but now Boomer is one of the most sought-after staff members for his ability to improve multiple social and emotional learning elements (SEL). I'm in my 25th year of college, and I believe in the need for social and emotional skills to be taught — they really help students succeed academically. I saw Boomer stopping a child's tears in record time, helping a school-phobic kindergarten teacher walk happily into school, resetting an anxious student's day, relieving test-taking anxiety, and giving smiles and laughter to everyone he encounters.

BRINGING IN A THERAPY DOG we were encouraged to pose questions and concerns when the District first considered getting us a therapy dog. And we did a pilot test with the high school therapy dog, Violet, before Boomer arrived, and considered her inclusion in the school to be highly helpful to our students. For example, when students were reading, Violet would join the English language arts class and teachers noticed that when she was present students were clearly more confident and took more chances in reading. Research clearly backs the advantages of dogs for therapy purpose our department cautiously measures the advantages and disadvantages of these dogs and determined the positives would outweigh the drawbacks. PAWS for People and Charlotte's Litter list the therapy dog's advantages. They can: reduce blood pressure and stress levels for people, raise dopamine and serotonin levels, and boost physical health. Reduce anxiety, increase positive mood significantly, promote social isolation and help kids develop social skills. Help young readers gain trust, after all the vaccinations had been issued, Boomer joined us at the beginning of the school year. He goes to one morning meeting of 20 minutes a day (rotating around the classrooms), and visits classes at certain times if he is asked by teachers. Students may also ask for time with Boomer— the teacher for advice, one of the two handlers, or I'll bring Boomer to the class or the student the come to us. In being present Boomer produces an aura of happiness. He's enthusiastic about meeting everyone and he's non-judgmental, kind to everyone and a great listener. His involvement helps students coping with problems related to friendship and family, school anxiety, and other problems. Students relax visibly when petting or playing with Boomer, and open up. The handlers have taken great steps to teach the students and staff on how to treat Boomer and connect. All students are required to watch a slideshow explaining the role of

Boomer in the school, how he was educated and how to approach him. We are taught the body language of dogs, and how to say whether Boomer is anxious, content, tired, or hungry. Such lessons are linked to the social and emotional skills that we cultivate in our students. We love Boomer, and take care of him.

DOGS ARE NOT FOR All But there are people who are opposed to having service dogs at school and have legitimate reasons about allergic reactions, pet care and dog anxiety. Addressing these issues, and providing open communication within the school community, is critical. Once we came to Boomer, we reached out to therapy dog schools and dog owners, and conducted research on dog allergies and dog anxiety in an attempt to address possible problems from the outset. Kids and adults who are afraid of dogs may have had a bad past encounter, or may not have ever been introduced to dogs. I have talked to the families of children who are afraid of dogs, and together we have developed strategies for various forms of handling them: they can want to be out of class while Boomer is around, or they may sit at or on a desk at the back of the school, or we can fully hold Boomer out of their school. Any students who want to sit on their desk shift forward when they see their peers playing with Boomer — most will pet him within a few class visits. One student was worried of dogs but decided to conquer his apprehension, and over a period of time one of Boomer's trainers worked with him. He will now pose next to Boomer. Allergies are also an important concern to tackle as no dogs are hypoallergenic and some dogs shed less than others. Parents consult with us on how and to what degree they want their child to be communicating with Boomer. We keep him on a leash in classrooms with allergic students to make sure he stays away from them, and we didn't have any issues with Boomer being present in a room for up to 40 minutes. For those of us who love dogs it is hard to accept that not everyone thinks the same way. Students are not expected to communicate with Boomer. We ask them to honor him and we understand their wish not to be next to him. The effect of this year's boomer on SEL has been big. When he's present, he has an immediate calming effect — students express thoughts and emotions more readily, for example, with guidance counselors and shy students come out of their shell. Definitely, the pros outweighed the contras.

Conclusion

The book consists entirely of specific guidelines for training a dog, whether for home training or for professional training purposes. Numerous methods are provided to train the dogs. As it was known training of a dog consists of different manual steps that need to be worked on. Others are training of dog to sit, stand, lie down, follow orders, eat food, remain focused, turn around, move, regulate emotions, and learn to track prey. Training of a dog is the utilization of behavioral analysis that uses antecedent and effects environmental factors to change the actions of the dog, either to assist it in particular exercises or to perform specific tasks, or to engage adequately in current household life. Although dogs training is for particular tasks somewhat goes back to the Roman period, training of dog to be friendly household pets evolved in the duration of 1950s with suburbanization. From experiences a dog can understand its surroundings. This can be by conventional practices from where it builds a connection among two stimulants, first one is not associative schooling from where its demeanor is changed through sensitization or habituation as well as operating practices and also where it builds a connection among a precedent including its effect. Several number of proven animal training techniques, each including its critics and adherents. The Koehler process, clicker training, incentive training, computer training, training of model-rival, training based on dominance, and training based on relationship are some of the best-known training of dog techniques. The typical aspects of effective approaches are knowledge of the strengths and temperament of the animal, precise timing of reward, regular communication and punishment. Punishment usage is contentious, with many behaviorists challenging both the morality and the efficacy. Household dogs have derived complicated traits from wolf predecessor, such as bite avoidance, that were packed hunters with a complicated body language. Such advanced modes of social communication and cognition might be the cause for their playfulness, skill to work in human homes, social settings and trainability, and such qualities gave dogs a human relationship that allowed them to be one of today's most popular species in the world. The importance of dogs to early human hunter-gatherers has managed dogs to become one of the most successful species on the planet. Dogs perform many things for individuals like herding, hunting, security, pulling loads, military and police aid, fellowship and lately helping people with disorders. Within the Western world, this impact on human culture has given them the nickname "A man's best buddy." Nevertheless, in some culture's dogs are also a meat source, too. Dogs have lived in many situations and served with humans. Besides the role of dogs as accompanying livestock, dogs were bred for cattle herding (collies, sheepdogs), hunting (hounds, pointers), and rodent control (terriers). Many types of working dogs include search and rescue dogs, tracking dogs equipped to detect illegal drugs or chemical weapons; dogs guarding; dogs helping fishermen use nets; and dogs pulling loads. Different types of service dogs and support dogs, including guide dogs, hearing dogs, mobility aid dogs, and therapeutic service dogs provide support to disabled people. It has been shown that certain dogs owned by epileptics warn their owner when the owner shows signs of an imminent seizure; often well in advance of the onset, allowing the guardian to seek protection, medication or medical attention.

Printed in Great Britain
by Amazon